Tarmacs and Trenches

Life and Disappearance of Lieutenant General Millard F. Harmon, Jr.

Robert G. Novotny

Tarmacs and Trenches

Life and Disappearance of Lieutenant General Millard F. Harmon, Jr.

Disclaimer

Acknowledgments

They say it is a cardinal sin to become attached to the subject of a biography. By doing so, the biographer may inflate the true impact of their subject or fail to identify his faults. I am not a professional biographer. During my research on Miff Harmon, I have come to respect the man he was, the leader he became, the warrior / fighter-pilot mentality he always had, and the loyalty he showed up and down the chain of command. I make no excuses, and I show no remorse for this tribute to him. I wanted to write this book simply to tell a story that needs to be told. One story of millions that happened but were lost while the world was at war.

Throughout my active duty career, my wife and children followed me around the globe while I chased my dream of being a fighter pilot. Despite crisscrossing the world, constant deployments, and several fortuitous promotions, I continually wondered if I was asking too much of them. To this question, my wife and best friend always answered, “Press.” The Lord has blessed me with an incredible family, more than I deserve.

The genesis of this paper was Dr. Tom Hughes. He brought the idea of writing about Miff to our School of Advanced Air and Space Studies class, and I jumped at the offer. Tom was a source of inspiration to me during the initial research and writing phases, not academically, as you might think, but rather in the department of courage. Thank you for introducing me to Miff. Likewise, I need to thank Dr. Rich Muller, whose keen eye and sage advice prevented many of my mistakes from going public and both of them graciously revisited this journey with me after 15 years in waiting.

Thank you to Millard F. 'Bud' Harmon, III, and Helen Harmon Nazzaro for sharing stories about their father. I am sorry I didn't complete this book in time, but I hope I honor your father.

Any errors in this are mine alone.

Table of Contents

Foreword i

Abstract iii

Chapter One: Disappearance 1

Chapter Two: A Pioneer Aviator Is Born 5

Learning From the Ground Up 9

Searching for Pancho 12

Chapter Three: The View from Above 18

Protecting the Canal 28

Chapter Four: School Days 31

Molding the Air Corps Tactical School 36

Changing the Rules 40

A Complete Overhaul 43

Fear of Change at the ACTS 50

Chapter Five: Witness to 'The Blitz' 55

Visions of the South Pacific 59

Chapter Six: The Road to War 67

Who's in Charge? 69

State of Affairs in the Pacific 74

Chapter Seven: Miff Harmon Strikes Back 84

"This Logistic Support Thing" 88

Hap Arnold's War by Algebra 90

Ghormley and the Battle on board the USS *Argonne* 97

Bull Halsey 105

Reinforcements Arrive 111

Lessons from Cactus 116

Chapter Eight: Forward Through the South Pacific 119

Attacked on Board the *McCawley* 125

Bougainville 130

Combat Fatigue in the Army Air Forces 133

Arnold Reassigns Twining 137

"Savage, Suicidal and Somewhat Stupid" 138

Harmon's Thoughts on SOPAC 141

A New Job 143

Chapter Nine: Navigating Treacherous Waters 145

Battling 'Big Army' 149

Putting Theory into Practice 151

Building the Foundation 153

XXI Bomber Command 156

The Importance of 'Box-ology' 161

Chapter Ten: Finishing Where He Started 164

From West Point to the Western Pacific 167

Power of Joint Operations 172

"Strategic Tenacity" 173

Arnold and Harmon 175

Lost in History 177

Bibliography ... 179

- Books ... 179
- Periodicals ... 181
- Newspaper Items ... 181
- Historical Studies ... 182
- Reports ... 182
- Unpublished Papers ... 182
- Letters ... 182
- Memorandums ... 187
- Summaries, Diaries, Minutes, Notes ... 188
- Addresses ... 189
- Electronic Publications ... 189

About the Author ... 190

Foreword

There are many characters from the annals of military history whose exploits simply deserve and demand attention, and General "Miff" Harmon is one of them. I freely digress that I wasn't familiar with the name when I began reading this, but the enthusiasm and meticulous attention to detail that went into compiling this excellent narrative was so remarkably compelling that I simply couldn't stop reading. I was very fortunate to meet the author, former Brigadier General Rob Novotny, some years ago when he and I appeared at the Four Seasons Hotel in Las Vegas at an event organized by our mutual friend ICC CEO Mr. Randy Garcia, and from that point on the die was cast.

Over the past fourteen years, I have published 14 books on the subject of military history and received a few Emmy Awards for my documentary work, which is extremely gratifying despite the fact that I didn't write any of these books to draw attention to myself. On the contrary, in fact, they're all about unsung heroes and divisions that were often overlooked or even ignored by history. I believe General "Miff" Harmon fits this profile, but hopefully, this work will go some way to amending this erroneous lapse.

His name should be synonymous with America's great aviators, such as Charles Lindbergh, Jimmy Doolittle, and Chuck Yeager, and this is precisely why you should read this. There are innumerable ways to present historical subject matter, but when someone, who was a fighter pilot himself, writes about the subject with fervor and passion, it will inevitably grip the reader. This is definitely the case here. The story will draw you in, engross, entertain, and enthrall you on all levels, and that is what it's all about. We have a tendency to forget that history was cast and molded by individuals and that it isn't just a sequence of names and events. It's about human beings. Human beings that transcended the parameters of day-to-day existence and raised the bar to meet frequently unimaginable, almost superhuman challenges.

To articulate and present the life of such a person as General "Miff" Harmon demands an extremely high level of dedication. I wouldn't expect anything less from former Brigadier General Rob Novotny, who is himself a war veteran, so it's safe to say that he knows his subject matter and then some. Its having had that experience that adds gravity and credulity to this narrative, which elevates this work to an absolute "must-read" status.

Remember your heroes, venerate your veterans, and when you proudly recall their names, including General "Miff" Harmon, he deserves that. Now all you must do is discover why, so I hope that you enjoy this as much as I did, and I'm sure that you will.

Martin King

Author of "Blood is Thicker Than War," and "Triage"

Abstract

Lieutenant General Millard F. Harmon, Jr. was the Commanding General of the Army Air Forces in the Pacific Oceans Area when he went missing in the Pacific on February 26, 1945. As AAFPOA, Harmon commanded one of the largest air organizations in history. Harmon's life as an airpower pioneer serves as a model for the modern, joint warfighting airman. Harmon began his career as a young infantry officer, graduating from the United States Military Academy. Within a few years, after transferring to the aviation section of the Army, Harmon flew in support of the Punitive Expedition in Mexico and over the hostile skies of Europe during World War I. In these formative years, Harmon formed life-long friendships with men who defined the United States Army and her air arm. Harmon commanded multiple organizations and air bases, including France Field, Panama Canal Zone, Barksdale Field, Louisiana, and Hamilton Field, California. Harmon spent two critical years serving as the Assistant Commandant of the Air Corps Tactical School. During his tenure, Harmon renovated an aging professional military education program and pushed for broad changes to the ACTS curriculum. Harmon advocated joint operational planning at ACTS, initiating several combined arms exercises with the nearby Infantry School.

Harmon served as a military observer to England and a special assistant to Mr. Averell Harriman, President Franklin Roosevelt's ambassador for military lend-lease activities to England. Harmon studied the Royal Air Force's model for war with emphasis on their air activities, recording the fine details for American military leaders. Following his assignment to England, the War Department called Harmon to lead all US Army forces in the South Pacific area, a largely US Navy theater. In the South Pacific, Harmon turned his attention to land combat activities, reinforcing Guadalcanal on several occasions while simultaneously building a South Pacific air force. Harmon and Admiral William F. "Bull" Halsey formed a lethal partnership as they synthesized many facets of combat power to expel the Japanese from the South Pacific. Halsey tasked Harmon several times to assume command of land combat operations on Guadalcanal, New Georgia, and Bougainville; a rare opportunity for a trained airman. Harmon achieved remarkable results as a land and air commander in the South Pacific. After nearly two years of commanding land forces, Harmon returned to his air roots and built a powerful air force from the Central Pacific Theater. Under the command of Admiral Chester W. Nimitz, Harmon worked diligently to navigate through incredibly complex and convoluted command arrangements while building the massive infrastructure required for B-29 operations against Japan.

Chapter One: Disappearance

I never had a parachute.
I never hope to see one.
But I'll tell you this much anyhow,
I hope I never need one.

Millard F. Harmon, Jr.

Shortly after sunset on February 26, 1945, callsign 68Y, a converted B-24D Liberator bomber, made its initial position report during the journey from Kwajalein in the Marshall Islands to Honolulu. The weather that evening was perfect for flying the longest leg between any two Pacific bases; from takeoff to landing, the 2,200 nautical mile flight would take a grueling fourteen hours.[1] A little less than four hours into the flight, the crew reported their position again this time however, the transmission was garbled and unreadable. It was also the last report from 68Y. Shortly after the plane was due in Hawaii, a combined air and sea search began. This search and rescue mission, which stretched across eighteen days and included over 3,500 aircraft sorties and numerous naval searches, was the largest ever conducted in World War II.[2] Nothing and no one was ever found in the vast ocean space. Commander in Chief Pacific Admiral Chester W. Nimitz discontinued the air search

---

[1] "Assembly" Association of Graduates, USMA, West Point Alumni Foundation, Inc., Newburgh, NY, Volume VII, No. 2 (July 1948), 13.

[2] "Report of Search for Lt.Gen. Millard F. Harmon, USAAF, Commanding General, Army Air Forces, Pacific Oceans Areas," March 1945, 702.293, IRIS No. 0250348, in Millard F. Harmon, Jr. Papers, Air Force Historical Research Agency (hereafter cited as AFHRA), 4.

on March 16th but ordered "transient ships and transient aircraft" to "continue to look out for survivors."[3] In one of many mysteries of World War II, three causes may explain the disappearance of 68Y: aircraft ditching due to a mechanical failure, destruction by a possible Japanese aircraft launched from a submarine, or, most probably, fuel fumes ignited by an electrical spark causing an explosion in flight.[4]

Ten people were on board 68Y when she disappeared that day. Her crew of six included Major Frank "Doc" Savage (pilot), First Lieutenant Jack West (co-pilot), Major Archibald Anderson (navigator), TSgt Steven Geist (radio operator), MSgt Douglas Anderson (engineer) and PFC Arthur Ofner (assistant engineer). There were four passengers on board 68Y, including TSgt McInery, Colonel William Ball, Brigadier General James Anderson, chief of staff to the Commanding General of Army Air Forces Pacific Oceans Area (AFFPOA), and the AFFPOA Commander himself, Lieutenant General Millard Fillmore Harmon, Jr., whose loss had motivated the enormous search operations.[5] General Harmon's responsibilities had included the organization, training, and equipping of all Army Air Forces in the Pacific Theater, a massive undertaking in peace let alone during war. In this capacity, he was responsible for over 208,000 personnel and hundreds of combat and support aircraft.[6] Few Army commanders in World War II had more personnel in a

---

[3] "Report of Search for Lt.Gen. Millard F. Harmon, USAAF, Commanding General, Army Air Forces, Pacific Oceans Areas," AFHRA, 5.
[4] "Report of Search for Lt.Gen. Millard F. Harmon, USAAF, Commanding General, Army Air Forces, Pacific Oceans Areas," AFHRA, 4.
[5] "Report of Search for Lt.Gen. Millard F. Harmon, USAAF, Commanding General, Army Air Forces, Pacific Oceans Areas," AFHRA, 5.
[6] Louis Morton, *United States Army in World War II, The War in the Pacific, Strategy and Command: The First Two Years* (1962; new imprint, Washington, DC: Center of Military History, 2000), 538.

combat zone under their command. Amazingly, General Harmon was neither a field army nor theater commander. General Harmon was an airman who had earlier led American ground forces during the initial operations of World War II and was, even as he went missing, tasked to organize the largest theater air force ever assembled.

Lieutenant General Millard F. Harmon, Jr. prepared and led America's young soldiers during the opening strokes of World War II. Throughout the darkest days of Guadalcanal, when victory was uncertain, Harmon took radical steps necessary to save the operation. Later, charged with the ground scheme of maneuver, Harmon orchestrated the successful campaigns on New Georgia and Bougainville. Finally, as combat operations in the South Pacific ebbed, Harmon was chosen to lead the largest combat air force ever assembled in the Pacific. As American air forces approached to within striking range of the Japanese homeland, Harmon provided the leadership and support necessary to develop a strategy for success.

Yet little has been written of Harmon's legacy. Harmon's role as a pioneer aviator, who helped in the formation of the Army Air Forces, his contributions to the successful campaigns through the Solomon Islands, and his final leadership role as the Americans approached the Japanese homeland have yet to be illuminated. Within his own service, Harmon did not receive the credit deserved for such victories. His final promotion and the majority of his wartime decorations stemmed from the endorsements of senior Navy, not Army officers. His dire requests for personnel and equipment during fierce fighting in the South Pacific went largely unfilled by an organization afraid of relinquishing too much power over its machines. Finally, as Americans prepared to deliver the fatal blow against their Pacific enemy, Harmon was intentionally trapped in a bureaucratic quagmire of unclear command relationships and senior officer power struggles. Nevertheless, throughout this entire time, Harmon never sacrificed his integrity or softened his quest for victory against Japan.

Much can be learned from General Harmon's life. During his thirty-five years of service, Harmon documented prescient lessons from major periods of conflict in American history. His keen insights regarding joint operations, command relationships and the warrior spirit still ring true today.

Chapter Two: A Pioneer Aviator Is Born

> Take a bulldog grip on the new occupation and never let go until your diploma is handed to you on graduation day in the grove in front of the chapel. After that happens take a new and maturer [sic] grip on the much more responsible duties of an officer [and] justify the belief, which I have expressed, that you will develop into an efficient army officer.

Millard F. Harmon, Sr., letter to Harmon, Jr. on his appointment to West Point, 4 November 1907

Fort Mason, in San Francisco, California, served as a key coastal defense battery in the Western United States. During many years of operations, Fort Mason also became a highly desired assignment for officers and their families in the Coastal Artillery of the United States Army. One such officer, First Lieutenant Millard Fillmore Harmon, was stationed at Fort Mason in January 1888 with his wife, Madeline, and their son Kenneth. On January 19th, the couple welcomed their second son, Millard Fillmore Harmon, Jr.

Millard Sr. was born on May 1, 1856 in Bedford County, Pennsylvania, and grew up in humble circumstances. Proud of his upbringing and grateful for his education at the United States Military Academy at West Point, Millard Sr. was a respected soldier and competent professional. An honor graduate of the Artillery School at Fort Monroe, Virginia, and later Professor of Military

Science and Tactics at the Pennsylvania Military Academy in Chester, Millard Sr. eventually rose to the rank of Colonel before retiring in 1914 just prior to the "Great War." Throughout his years, Millard Sr. was considered an "ardent sportsman in the truest sense," preferring to spend time outdoors fishing, hunting, and exploring, all skills he eventually taught to his three sons, Kenneth, Millard Jr., and Hubert.[7]

Figure 1: West Point Ice Hockey Team of 1910. Cadet Miff Harmon seated far left in the front row. Source: Millard F. Harmon, III. Picture in the author's collection.

Millard Jr. acquired the moniker Miff at an early age. Like his father, he enjoyed everything about the outdoors. Fishing, hunting, and sporting exploits characterized his childhood. Harmon's

[7] Most of this paragraph is referenced from the "Sixty-First Annual Report of the Association of Graduates of the United States Military Academy at West Point, New York: June 11, 1930," Millard Fillmore Harmon obituary, Newburgh, NY: The Moore Printing Company, Inc., 149 – 152.

athletic career continued to excel following his acceptance to West Point in 1908. Miff's size was average: five foot eight inches tall and about one hundred and fifty pounds. Yet this did not deter him from playing two of the roughest team sports offered at the Point, lacrosse, and ice hockey. Known as somewhat of a "runt," Miff combined a quiet style and "aggressive and skillful stick work" to dazzle opponents, hit when he needed to, and impress his teammates.[8] He captained the varsity ice hockey team for two straight years while continuing to participate in an assortment of other predominantly outdoor activities.

Academically, Harmon did not have as much success. Throughout his four years attending West Point, his class standing was never impressive. During his second year at the academy, his class order of merit was 82nd of 98 total students, eventually rising to 74th of 96 by the time he graduated in 1912. Miff's courses at West Point included Mathematics, English, History, French, Spanish, Law, Drill, Practical Military Engineering, Drawing, and Military Hygiene.[9] His grades in these courses were barely adequate throughout his student career, though he did tolerably well in Drawing and Military Hygiene. In Drawing, he finished in the solid middle of his class at the 61st percentile. The Drawing class at West Point taught students the basics of freehand design. Later, students brought their knowledge of geometry and the use of drawing implements to create topographical maps and military landscape sketches. The course emphasized architecture,

---

[8] "Assembly," Association of Graduates, USMA, West Point Alumni Foundation, Inc., Newburgh, NY, Volume VII, No. 2 (July 1948): 12.

[9] United States Military Academy, "Official Register for the Officers and Cadets, United States Military Academy for 1912," West Point, NY: United States Military Academy Printing Office, 1912, 14. http://digital-library.usma.edu/libmedia/archives/oroc/v1912.pdf (accessed 20 Jan 2007).

assessment of geography, and the ability to read and write construction plans.[10]

His strongest course of study was Military Hygiene, where he finished in the top third of all students. The Military Hygiene course consisted of six lectures, thirteen recitations, and a summer camp exercise which required cadets to demonstrate an understanding of the hazards of austere troop encampment conditions and to determine actions to prevent infectious diseases and sanitation problems with an emphasis on first-aid procedures. Designed with future commanders in mind, the Military Hygiene course was developed to teach cadets the methods and procedures that would preserve the Army's greatest resource, military manpower.[11]

Athletics and academics aside, Miff Harmon graduated from West Point as a well-respected and honorable young Army officer. Classmates remembered him as a "stout-hearted loyal friend who knew his own mind and never hesitated to carry out what he considered right, regardless of the opposition."[12] Cadet Harmon's loyalty, personal conviction, and strong self-confidence were evident in the classroom and in the fields of athletic competition. His classmates further remembered Miff for his organizational expertise, tolerance and understanding of others, and unvarying consideration for the welfare of the members of his team, especially those junior in grade. These personal traits, solidified at West Point, weave throughout Miff's assignments during his

---

[10] "Official Register for the Officers and Cadets, United States Military Academy for 1912," 66, (accessed 20 Jan 2007).
[11] "Official Register for the Officers and Cadets, United States Military Academy for 1912," 68, (accessed 20 Jan 2007).
[12] "Assembly," USMA, West Point Alumni Foundation, 12.

remarkable career. An authentic leader, competent teammate, and someone who could be counted on when times were toughest.

Learning From the Ground Up

Upon graduation from West Point, Harmon was commissioned a Second Lieutenant on June 12, 1912 and assigned to the Infantry branch of the US Army. For the next three years, Harmon learned the basics of Infantry organization, management of troops, and modern battlefield tactics. The Army stationed Harmon at the 28th Infantry Regiment at Fort Snelling, Minnesota, from September 12, 1912 until February 6, 1913. He then transferred to the 9th Infantry Regiment at Fort Thomas, Kentucky, for one year. His unit moved to Laredo, Texas, and until November 30, 1914, Miff conducted patrol operations along the contentious US-Mexico border. On December 1st, Harmon moved to the 24th Infantry Regiment, then in the Philippines serving at Camp McGrath, Batangas, PI, and Camp Eldridge, Laguna, P.I. Both McGrath and Eldridge camps, located in Southern Luzon, were in an area that had been rife with enemy guerrilla activity only a few years before during the Philippine War. As a foot soldier in the Philippines, Harmon had first-hand experience with the difficult conditions common to tropical Pacific islands. Heat, humidity, and torrential typhoons were commonplace, as well as debilitating insect-borne diseases such as malaria, encephalitis, typhoid, and smallpox.[13] The lack of adequate water treatment facilities, in particular, kept soldiers on constant watch for cholera and dysentery outbreaks.[14]

---

[13] Brian McAllister Linn, *The Philippine War: 1899-1902* (Lawrence, KS: University Press of Kansas, 2000), 16.

[14] Note: Harmon's father served in the Philippine campaign in 1898 as a member of the 13th Minnesota Volunteers (source: Maj Gen Harmon military biography, August 7, 1941, 168.604-15, IRIS No. 00124146, AFHRA).

The Philippine archipelago covers nearly one-half million square miles on over 7,000 individual islands. Those islands are further divided by mountain ranges, swamps, and jungles, creating diverse pockets of non-homogeneous peoples.[15] The islands host several languages and cultures, which further complicate any foreigner's ability to deal with local circumstances. During the Philippine War, the US Army had dispatched nearly 70,000 troops to help quell fighting in this island chain, and this force was insufficient for the task. The Army faced serious problems with terrain, poor communications, a lack of cultural expertise, inadequate logistical infrastructure, and disease, in addition to armed resistance.[16] Limited forward spotting crippled any long-range firepower. Americans in the Philippines learned lessons the hard way. Miff's Philippine experience, coming shortly after that regional war, where these lessons were still fresh, laid the foundation for an appreciation of the difficult nature of land warfare in tropical Pacific areas, conditions that would reappear in the South Pacific during World War II.

It was also in the Philippines that Harmon got his initial appreciation for military aviation. In August 1911, the Chief Signal Officer of the Army recommended the establishment of an air station in the Philippines to conduct maneuvers with infantry units assigned to the islands. By that December, a single aircraft and a handful of personnel were on their way to the Philippines, where they established the Philippine Air School the following March. Although the school was plagued by accidents, safety closures, and monsoon rains, Philippine Air School pilots traveled extensively

---

[15] Linn, *The Philippine War*, 15.
[16] Linn, *The Philippine War*, 325.

around the islands, demonstrating the early efficacy of American airpower with regard to maneuver, aerial surveying and logistics.

Immediately prior to the outbreak of World War I, the Army Air Service sent another young aviator to the Philippines to participate in a large series of maneuvers near Batangas. Lieutenant Henry H. 'Hap' Arnold, future five star general and Commanding General of the United States Army Air Forces, arrived in the Philippines in 1914 to participate in an exercise that simulated a Japanese landing along Batangas beaches defended by the US and Philippine forces.[17] In what would be the start of a long professional relationship, Arnold and Harmon met in the Philippines and firmly rooted themselves as friends destined to be pioneer aviators.[18]

Harmon's time in the Philippines exposed him to the Aviation Section of the Signal Corps and fostered a developing desire to fly. Although the Philippine Air School closed in January 1915 following the destruction of its last aircraft, the thrill of flight had sown the seeds of curiosity in Miff's mind, and he immediately requested a transfer to aviation.[19] War Department officials approved his request about the time he returned to the US in 1915. He was promoted to First Lieutenant on July 1, 1916 and graduated from flight training on October 15th with the rating of Junior Military Aviator. Shortly thereafter, Harmon achieved the rating of Military Aviator, which According to War Department Bulletin No. 2, was awarded to those personnel able to "attain an altitude of at least 2,500 feet, fly in a 15-mile-per-hour wind, carry a passenger to a height of at least 500 feet and immediately make a dead-stick

---

[17] H. H. Arnold, *Global Mission* (New York: Harper & Brothers Publishers, 1949), 44.
[18] Arnold, *Global Mission*, 338.
[19] "Assembly," USMA, West Point Alumni Foundation, 12.

landing within 150 feet of a previously designated point, and make a military reconnaissance cross-country flight of at least 20 miles at an average altitude of 1,500 feet."[20] While primitive by today's aviation standards, the attainment of such skill in the early twentieth century warranted due recognition.

Searching for Pancho

Following his flight training, the Army returned Harmon to the US-Mexico border to join a fledgling aviation unit. Columbus, New Mexico, had been making headlines around the United States before October 1916 when he arrived in the 1st Aero Squadron. On March 9, 1916, a band of approximately 750 Mexican revolutionaries led by Francisco "Pancho" Villa crossed into the United States and killed seventeen Americans in Columbus.[21] One week later, under orders from President Woodrow Wilson, Brigadier General John J. "Black Jack" Pershing led the Punitive Expedition into Mexico to either kill or capture the revolutionary leader. While Pershing's forces were assembling, the 1st Aero Squadron commander, Captain Benjamin D. Foulois, received orders to assist Pershing's main effort. Under-staffed and ill-prepared, the 1st Aero Squadron and young aviator Miff Harmon crossed into Mexico and entered unforeseen territory.

---

[20] Juliette A. Hennessy, *The United States Army Air Arm, April 1861 to April 1917*, USAF Historical Study 98 (Maxwell AFB, AL: USAF Historical Division, Air University, 1958), 59.

[21] Hennessy, *The United States Army Air Arm*, 167.

Harmon joined the unit toward the end of the Punitive Expedition but deployed forward to operating locations approximately 120 miles south of Columbus near Colonia Dublán and El Valle, Mexico.[22] Also in the unit with Harmon during this expedition were Lieutenants Ralph Royce and Carl "Tooey" Spaatz, men who formed alliances with Miff for the rest of their lives.[23] Spaatz would later go on to become the first Chief of Staff of the United States Air Force in 1947. These men, along with other pilots and maintenance personnel, were equipped with eight Curtiss JN3 'Jenny' aircraft, a handful of trucks, and an automobile.[24]

Figure 2: 1st Aero Squadron on the Mexican Border. Source: US Army Transportation Museum Site, "War on Wheels: Mexican – Punitive Expedition – 1916." Source: http://www.transchool.eustis.army.mil/Museum/MexWar.htm (accessed 5 May 2007).

As the inaugural combat aviation unit of the United States to enter battle, the 1st Aero Squadron was not ready to face three major challenges during the next year. First, the squadron operated in incredibly harsh conditions. On the ground, pilots and support personnel were required to work grueling hours to keep their limited fleet in operation. The limited payload capacity of the JN3s

[22] United States Military Academy, Biographical Register of the Officers and Graduates of USMA, Volume 6B, Part 3, Cullum 5091, 1920.
[23] Hennessy, *The United States Army Air Arm*, 167.
[24] Hennessy, *The United States Army Air Arm*, 167.

meant pilots routinely flew without adequate clothing, food, or water. During their long missions, pilots and their aircraft were exposed to high winds, rain, snow, and hail, all of which, "because of inadequate clothing, invariably caused excessive suffering."[25] Crash landings were routine during the Punitive Expedition, fortunately causing only minor injuries. Still, a growing lack of faith in their flying machines caused mental anguish for many of the aviators.[26]

Second, the aircraft were not up to the requirements of the mission. At the beginning of the Punitive Expedition, the 1st Aero Squadron possessed eight older Curtis JN3s. These aircraft had already been in service for quite some time and were hardly ready for sustained combat operations.[27] The primary missions of the aircraft and pilots were to conduct observation, reconnaissance, limited theater airlift, and rudimentary surface attacks. Sorties flown into Mexico were longer than most training sorties, increasing the demands on the aging aircraft.

Additionally, due to the mountainous terrain, the aircraft needed to perform many functions above 10 – 12,000 feet.[28] Poor compasses, bad maps, and unfamiliarity with the local terrain made observation flights difficult for the young pilots. These conditions conspired with strong mountain winds and turbulent air currents, forcing many pilots to make emergency landings in the middle of the barren landscape, sometimes damaging aircraft beyond repair.[29]

---

[25] Hennessy, *The United States Army Air Arm*, 173.
[26] Hennessy, *The United States Army Air Arm*, 173.
[27] Hennessy, *The United States Army Air Arm*, 167.
[28] Hennessy, *The United States Army Air Arm*, 168.
[29] Calvin W. Hines, "First Aero Squadron in Mexico," *American Aviation Historical Journal* 10, no. 3 (3rd Quarter 1965): 194.

In the air and on the ground, the harsh climate extracted a high toll on the Jennies. The dry, arid southwest wreaked havoc on canvas materials and caused wooden propellers to crack and virtually "fly apart" without warning.[30] At the conclusion of the flying day, pilots and maintenance personnel removed propellers and stored them in humidors, but this was but a poor remedy.[31] After a few months of operations, only two of the original eight Jennies were still in service.[32]

Third, the supply system and pace of replacement parts and personnel were too slow. During the opening months of the Punitive Expedition, Foulois sent multiple memoranda to Pershing asking for replacement parts and newer, more capable aircraft. Eventually, the tempo of combat operations and the unforgiving environment forced the 1st Aero Squadron to its culminating point. By April 1916, with a growing war in Europe and a faltering expedition into Mexico, Congress passed the Urgent Deficiency Act. From that legislation, the 1st Aero Squadron was authorized twelve new aircraft for combat use. Soon Foulois found four Curtiss N8 airplanes, exactly the aircraft he did not want. Foulois knew and later demonstrated the inability of the N8s to accomplish the missions required of the 1st Aero Squadron in Mexico. Deemed unsuitable for use in the Mexican theater, the Curtiss N8 was nevertheless the only plane available at the time. Over the next few months, other aircraft types would make their way to Columbus, but none would prove adequate.

---

[30] Arnold, *Global Mission*, 45.
[31] Hennessy, *The United States Army Air Arm,* 169.
[32] Air and Space Power Journal, Mexican Punitive Expedition (Maxwell AFB, AL: Air University Press, 2002), http://www.airpower.maxwell.af.mil/airchronicles/apj /apj02/win02/notam4.pdf (accessed 4 February 2007).

The Punitive Expedition into Mexico underscored the hurdles combat airpower faced at the dawn of the air age. During this baptism by fire, Miff Harmon and the other young aviators learned three significant lessons. First, it was evident that the Army lacked an appropriate observation aircraft. Based on the experiences in Mexico, an observation aircraft needed to hold two crewmembers, a pilot and an observer. This meant the aircraft needed a powerful engine, a sufficient living environment for its crew, and better navigational equipment. Second, close coordination with friendly ground forces and familiarity with the mission, terrain, and the enemy were crucial for operational success. Too often, pilots of the 1st Aero Squadron were unable to identify friendly units from enemy forces or discriminate Mexican civilians and bandits, a challenge for modern aviators even today.[33] Inadequate topographical maps combined with a poor understanding of the ground scheme of maneuver resulted in wasted sorties and inadequate observation reports. Finally, field conditions in an expeditionary setting were extremely harsh and took a greater-than-expected toll on the men and equipment. Climate, terrain, routine, and hostile actions drove the 1st Aero Squadron's aircraft into the ground and forced a decrease in operations during critical moments in the Expedition.

Major Foulois summarized his units' experiences in his "Report of Operations of the First Aero Squadron." "The experience gained by the commissioned and enlisted personnel of this command while on active duty with the Punitive Expedition," Foulois reported, "has been of the greatest value, and it is believed that the knowledge gained by all concerned should result in a more

---

[33] Herbert A. Johnson, *U.S. Army Aviation through World War I* (Chapel Hill, NC: The University of North Carolina Press, 2001), 168.

rapid and efficient development of the aviation service in the US Army."[34]

Despite the limited success of Pershing's Punitive Expedition into Mexico, the aviation arm of the US Army again took a step forward in their development. 1st Aero Squadron aviators displayed raw bravery irrespective of any broader implications for airpower. Facing a grueling environment in untrustworthy aircraft, the men of the 1st Aero Squadron performed their missions with great skill and incredible courage. The military aviators of the 1st Aero Squadron, including Carl Spaatz, Ralph Royce, Benjamin Foulois, and Miff Harmon, solidified their status as air pioneers in the US Army. Having earned their wings prior to World War I, these men would, in the future, nurture airpower and rise to command more flyers in battle.

---

[34] "Report of Operations of the First Aero Squadron, Signal Corps, with Punitive Expedition" by Benjamin D. Foulois, 28 August 1916, 168.65011-7A, AFHRA, 6.

Chapter Three: The View from Above

> "Aviation is fine as a sport. But as an instrument of war, it is worthless."
>
> *General Ferdinand Foch, Professor of Strategy, 1911*

> "It had been conclusively shown that aviation was a dominant element in the making of war even in the comparatively small way in which it was used by the armies in Europe."
>
> *Brigadier General William 'Billy' Mitchell Winged Defense*

After his time in Mexico, Harmon's military career accelerated along with the technology in the machines he was flying. With little time to recover, the War Department ordered him to travel to Europe and fight in World War I along with the French escadrilles. Harmon served as a Technical Advisor in the Army Air Service, learning what he could from the French so he could infuse those lessons into American combat practices. Before departing for Europe, he eloped with California socialite Alberta Beatrice Clark. A friend and fellow aviator, Harold Clark, had introduced Harmon to his sister during Miff's introductory flight training in North Island, San Diego. Following a whirlwind honeymoon and a brief stop in Washington, DC, Miff sailed for France on April 6, 1917. By the third week in April, Harmon was in Paris, where he enrolled in French aviation schools to learn to fly Spads, Nieuports, and other European machines. While in the French schools, the Army promoted Miff to Captain in the Infantry and then Major (temporary) in the Aviation Section of the Signal Corps, all on May 15th. Major Harmon's aviation talents set him apart in the French schools. The Commandant of the Military Aviation School of Pau remarked that Harmon "show[ed] excellent aptitude for making a pursuit pilot" with "a great deal of 'go.'"[35]

Figure 3: Harmon in France – 1918. Colonel Billy Mitchell is seated in the first row, third from the left. Harmon is seated in the first row, third from the right, leaning forward. Source: Millard F. Harmon, III. Picture in the author's collection.

Upon graduation from the French schools in June 1917, Harmon's first assignment took him to Chaumont as the Assistant to the Aviation Officer in the American Expeditionary Force (AEF).[36] Shortly after arriving at the AEF headquarters, the Army detailed

---

[35] "Certificate of Aptitude" by Military Aviation School of Pau, 28 May 1917, 168.604-10, IRIS No. 00124140, in Personal Papers of M.F. Harmon, Jr., Major Air Service Advisory Board, 1917 – 1921, AFHRA.

[36] United States Military Academy, Biographical Register of the Officers and Graduates of USMA, Volume 6B, Part 3, Cullum 5091, 1920.

Harmon to a temporary two-man board that was to verify the piloting skills of fellow Americans in France. One such pilot was William 'Billy' Mitchell, who had been unable to retrieve his aviation certificates from the States. Mitchell would eventually rise to the rank of Brigadier General and is widely regarded as the father of the Air Force. Harmon observed Mitchell fly and approved his rating as a Junior Military Aviator. The board report concluded Mitchell had "handled his machine with ease and very good control... and is well qualified in every way to be rated as a junior military aviator."[37] Mitchell, who was serving as a senior officer at the AEF headquarters, aimed to surround himself with keen aviators, tireless workers, and officers with "the most daring spirits."[38] Mitchell recognized Harmon fit this mold perfectly and assigned him to his personal staff at Chaumont.

Later, Harmon traveled extensively throughout Europe, studying French aviation organizations, tactics, and administration. He toured aviation units, met with commanders and pilots, inspected artillery fortifications, and spent time in the trenches. Initially, the land war in Europe was characterized by the "rapid advances and flanking movements" of a maneuver war that promised to pose significant problems for observation efforts from the sky.[39] However, by early summer 1917, when Harmon took to the skies over Northern France, the war had transformed into trench warfare and a static battlefront. As part of his duties, Harmon secured an observation sortie on June 9, 1917 in a French Farman aircraft from the 203 Escadrille and headed for the front

---

[37] Burke Davis, *The Billy Mitchell Affair* (New York: Random House, 1967), 29.
[38] Davis, *The Billy Mitchell Affair*, 36.
[39] Herbert A. Johnson, *U.S. Army Aviation through World War I* (Chapel Hill, NC: The University of North Carolina Press, 2001), 141.

lines.[40] In his notes, he commented on how the "soil is of a chalk formation, and it is remarkable how distinct the trenches appear. They are like irregular white streaks of paint on a green field."[41] Harmon also noted the great difficulty facing observation pilots. "Besides the gigantic trench construction," Harmon wrote, "perhaps the most remarkable thing is the great attention given to camouflage. Everything, except the trenches, is 'camouflé' from airplanes."[42]

Figure 4: Harmon during World War I. Harmon (left) with Colonel George C. Marshall (center) and General John J. "Black Jack" Pershing (right). Source: Millard F. Harmon, III. Picture in the author's collection.

As with earlier experiences, Harmon learned the distinct realities of war on the ground and war in the sky. The relatively

---

[40] "Carnet d' Emploi du Temps," by M.F. Harmon Jr., in Millard F. Harmon, Jr. Papers, 168.604-7, IRIS No. 00124135, AFHRA. (Hereafter cited as "Carnet d' Emploi du Temps").

[41] "Notes of trip to the French Front in the Region of Chalons sur-Marne – June 1917," by Millard F. Harmon, Jr., June 1917, in Millard F. Harmon, Jr. Papers, 168.604-6, IRIS No. 00124134, AFHRA, 7 – 8. (Hereafter cited as "Notes of trip to the French Front").

[42] Harmon, Notes of trip to the French Front, 21.

sterile air environment was violent and dangerous yet paled in comparison to the horrors below. Aviation's contribution to the man on the ground required accurate and timely observation reports. Maneuver units on the ground depended on their aviation comrades above to help make sense of the trench warfare madness all around them.

The answer to observation challenges came in a robust reconnaissance effort by the French. Harmon noted that "the trenches are constantly photographed so that any changes or additions will be known. They are now using a monoplane Spad for this purpose, and very good results are obtained," he wrote.[43] "These photographs are very clear and are invaluable."[44] Harmon further elaborated toward the end of his report that "it will be readily seen that there is a vast importance to photography and it is imperative that the photographs and observers be well trained and that the equipment be good."[45] One hundred years later, not much has changed. Counterinsurgency efforts in the Middle East or Afghanistan not only depended on accurate and timely surveillance from the air, but birthed a robust mission set for the Air Force. The introduction of MQ-1 Predator and MQ-9 Reaper unmanned systems, along with the plethora of other classes of drones, has significantly aided the soldier's mission on the ground.

Harmon also mentioned three important characteristics of the French effort: infantry liaison, Escadrille operating procedures, and aviation discipline. Harmon believed aviation coordination with infantry forces was crucial. He noted that liaison with the land forces is "carried out during an attack and consists in as close a

---

[43] Harmon, Notes of trip to the French Front, 28.
[44] Harmon, Notes of trip to the French Front, 28.
[45] Harmon, Notes of trip to the French Front, unnumbered page.

cooperation with infantry as possible."[46] This observation reinforced Harmon's personal experiences during the Punitive Expedition when aviators had difficulty distinguishing between American units and Mexican bandits.

Harmon also noted the unique organizational dynamic between the aviation section and the infantry commander. After visiting numerous infantry and artillery units at the front, he wrote about his conversations with the land commanders. "In regard to the Corps d' Armee Esqadrilles [sic] operation," Harmon reported, "one thing he mentioned is that the Commandant of the Aviation Group has the final 'say' as to whether the airplanes will operate or not. The General or Colonel cannot force the airplanes to operate against the judgment of the Chief de Group or Squadron. This is one of the many reasons why this chief should be an experienced aviator."[47]

Finally, Harmon witnessed a disturbing event toward the end of his initial tour of the French Front that led him to emphasize the need for discipline and professionalism in the field of aviation. During his final reported period, he returned to one of the Escadrille bases, where he witnessed an aerial demonstration that turned into a tragedy.

"Pausard and another Lieut. gave a wonderful exhibition of aerobatic work. Pausard is one of the foremost French "Aces." He has a record of 16 Bosches.[48] At the end of his exhibition, he passed

---

[46] Harmon, Notes of trip to the French Front, 29.

[47] Harmon, Notes of trip to the French Front, unnumbered page, author's emphasis.

[48] Bosches or Boches is a French slang term used during World War I when referring to the Germans. There are a variety of spelling variations. It means, loosely translated, pig-headed, blockheaded or stubborn. Americans picked up

down the field about twenty feet high and about twenty feet from the General. At the end of the field, he attempted to make an abrupt ascending turn and land in the opposite direction. His speed was so great, however, that his machine fished through the air instead of answering to the controls, and he crashed to the ground, smashing his machine to splinters and injuring himself badly. At this hour, it is not known whether he will live or not. It is very sad and a great loss to the cause."[49]

In response to this accident, Harmon condemned the practice of performing aerobatics below two thousand feet. He also wrote that aviation was still a hazardous occupation and demanded great respect for the machine. "It is very essential that the Chasse[50] man be an expert with his machine gun and also that he be expert in acrobatic works," he wrote. "To outmaneuver the enemy, he must have perfect control of his machine and do with it what he will."[51]

After touring the French lines, Harmon spent a short visit with the British in July 1917, taking part in a night bombing mission on board a Handley Page aircraft. He then returned to Hill 402, the airfield adjacent to the AEF Headquarters at Chaumont, where he continued to fly Spad and Nieuport aircraft while working on the headquarters staff.[52] In March 1918, Miff Harmon returned to

---

this term during World War I and were said to have put the 'Kibosh' on the Germans.

[49] Harmon, Notes of trip to the French Front, unnumbered page.

[50] 'Chasse' pilots were equivalent to American pursuit / fighter pilots.

[51] Harmon, Notes of trip to the French Front, unnumbered page.

[52] Harmon's logbook details exactly the types of aircraft and the motors. He frequently commented on the power of each airplane and their performance. Aircraft he flew include Nieuport 10, 13, 15, 18, 23 and 28, Spad 140 and 180, Mauric Farman Biplanes and Handley Page Bombers with the English. He flew with several different Escadrilles as an American advisor but predominantly Groupe de Combat #13 near Coincy.

Figure 5: Spad #134: Flown extensively by Harmon during World War I. According to Harmon's WWI logbook, Harmon visited units and maintained his currencies in this aircraft. Source: Photo courtesy of Alan Toelle. Picture in the author's collection.

flying combat missions over the front lines. With the looming American intervention and the belief that fresh forces could swing the balance in favor of the allies, German air activity increased.

Millard Harmon flew several combat missions over the front lines and grappled with German aircraft on a few occasions. On March 8, 1918, Harmon noted in his logbook a "dogfight" against a single German aircraft.[53] The German machine spun out of control during the fight and crashed, yet, authorities did not credit Harmon with a victory.[54] On the following day, Harmon, Davenport Johnson, and James Miller, commander of the 95th Aero Squadron, embarked on a sweep mission to destroy enemy aircraft.[55] Almost immediately after takeoff, Harmon's engine began to fail, and he returned to base, logging only a ten-minute flight.[56]

---

[53] Harmon, Carnet d' Emploi du Temps.
[54] Harmon, Carnet d' Emploi du Temps.
[55] Harmon, Carnet d' Emploi du Temps.
[56] Harmon, Carnet d' Emploi du Temps.

Figure 6: Harmon with Allied Officers. Major Harmon pictured with numerous allied officers in France. Harmon is seated in the front row, tenth from the left, holding the side of the French flag (#18). Davenport Johnson is believed to be in the front row, seventh from the left (#15). Date unknown. Source: Photo courtesy of Alan Toelle. Picture in the author's collection.

Johnson and Miller continued forward, engaging several enemy aircraft. At some point in the mission, enemy forces shot Miller down behind German lines.[57] There is some historical confusion regarding Johnson's actions that day, and Harmon's logbook does not add much clarity to the episode.[58] Johnson and Harmon flew

---

[57] Harmon, Carnet d' Emploi du Temps.

[58] Many internet theorists claim that Davenport Johnson either failed to act in an attempt to save Miller's life during his engagement or fled the engagement from the beginning. Some sites have referred to him as 'Jam' Johnson referring to Johnson's claim that his machine guns jammed thus preventing him from intervening. Harmon's logbook states: "Started on patrol with Johnson and Miller. Motor trouble. J + M went out alone. Miller down in (unreadable – xxreille) inside Bosches Lines. N.J. Fines. No confirmation as yet." Davenport Johnson would later participate in the St Mihiel and *Argonne* actions in World War I and eventually rise to the rank of Major General before retiring in November 1945.

another combat mission the next day, and eventually, Johnson took command of the 95th Aero Squadron that summer.

Air activity, as well as surface combat, reached a crescendo during the third week of March 1918, when the Germans launched the Spring Offensive. Harmon flew extensively during this period, logging fifteen combat missions with almost twenty-one combat hours in just fifteen days.[59] According to Harmon's son, Millard F. Harmon III, the Army credited Miff with the downing of several barrage balloons during this period.[60] For his contributions and bravery during World War I, the French government awarded Harmon the Croix de Guerre with bronze star. According to the French commander, Major Brocard, Commander of Combat Wing No. 2, Harmon served as a pilot with Spa Escadrille 65 and was considered an "officer of great conscientiousness and splendid courage. Having entered a French Escadrille for instruction, he has persisted in taking part in all the patrols of this Escadrille and, in addition, has made a great many voluntary patrols, thus giving the finest example of enthusiasm and disregard of danger."[61]

After weeks of combat air patrols, Harmon returned to AEF Headquarters and began work on a special commission to investigate future aerodrome sites, aircraft engine types, and airframe design for use in 1919, should the war continue. This work only lasted one month when the Army recalled him home after nearly eighteen months overseas.

---

[59] Harmon, Carnet d' Emploi du Temps.

[60] Millard F. Harmon, III (Son of Miff Harmon), interviewed by the author, 17 February 2007.

[61] Croix de Guerre Citation, Squadron Order No. 56, 9816-C, First Aeronautical Division, Combat Wing No. 2 Staff, translated by Chief of Air Service, French Mission, no date, from Millard F. Harmon, III, in the author's personal collection.

Upon returning to the United States, Harmon served in Washington, DC, in the office of the Director of the Air Service. His jobs included Chief of Flying Branch, Training Section, and then Assistant Chief of the Training Section before taking command of the 1st Provisional Wing in Minneola, Long Island, in October 1918. During his tour in Washington, the Army promoted Harmon twice in three months: Major (permanent) on June 7, 1918 and Lieutenant Colonel (temporary) on August 20, 1918.[62]

Protecting the Canal

After only nine months in the United States, Harmon, with Alberta, returned overseas as commander of France Field and Department Air Officer in the Panama Canal Zone in February 1919.[63] The Panama Canal, officially opened in August 1914, was, from the outset, recognized as a strategic interest of the United States. Prior to Harmon's arrival, Army and Naval Air Service aircraft conducted vast maritime patrols well out to sea in continuous protective efforts.[64] During World War I, flight conditions around Panama were difficult, and "happily no losses were sustained," Harmon wrote in his notes.[65] Harmon further wrote the successful execution of those patrol missions was due in part to the "courage and efficiency" of the Air Service pilots. "Great credit is also due those indomitable NCOs," Harmon wrote, "who

---

[62] United States Military Academy, Biographical Register of the Officers and Graduates of USMA, Volume 6B, Part 3, Cullum 5091, 1920.

[63] An article in the Honolulu Advertiser, August 1937, written by William Ewing stated Harmon was responsible for the opening of France Field. As of this writing, this claim is unknown.

[64] Untitled notes regarding a topographical survey of Panama by Millard F. Harmon, Jr., undated, 168-604-2, IRIS No. 00124140, in Millard F. Harmon, Jr. Papers, AFHRA. (Hereafter cited as "Topographical survey notes").

[65] Harmon, Topographical survey notes.

drove up and down the coast thru the heavy seas and tropical storms... to safeguard the lives of their pilots, observers, and mechanics."[66]

When he arrived at France Field, Harmon conducted a thorough review of the airdrome and the surrounding locations. In a handwritten, undated journal, Harmon used his experiences from World War I and the Mexican Punitive Expedition to identify critical issues affecting operations under his command. Not surprisingly, only non-aviators had commanded France Field prior to Miff Harmon's appearance.[67] In his notes, he wrote Panama had "never been flown over, [and] it had never been prospected from an aviation standpoint, and that [previous commanders] were... unfamiliar with the requirements for a landing field."[68] Harmon used his keen aviation experience and significant combat background to survey the entire Panama Canal Zone with the design of improving air operations in the region. Additionally, he was able to orchestrate several Army Air Service and Naval Air Service exercises, increasing the joint exchange of information.

Unfortunately, the tragic loss of a friend and fellow military aviator pierced Harmon's Panama Canal Zone tour. On May 2, 1919, while flying on an Army seaplane, Major Harold Clark's aircraft engine failed, and his plane crashed in the Mira Flores Locks, throwing his body from the plane to the bottom of the Panama Canal.[69] Clark was a seasoned military aviator, earning his wings in 1916 along with Miff Harmon. Together they had been

---

[66] Harmon, Topographical survey notes.
[67] Harmon, Topographical survey notes.
[68] Harmon, Topographical survey notes.
[69] Arlington National Cemetery Website, "Harold Melville Clark, Major, United States Army Air Service," http://www.arlingtoncemetery.net/hmclark.htm (accessed 10 February 2007).

assigned to the 1st Aero Squadron and flew in the Punitive Expedition before parting ways. The military assigned Clark to Hawaii (becoming the first pilot to fly in the islands), Washington, DC, San Diego, and New York before reuniting with Lieutenant Colonel Harmon in Panama. Based on his position as commander of France Field and the fact that Harold Clark was his brother-in-law, Miff Harmon escorted Clark home to be buried in Arlington National Cemetery.[70]

During the interwar period, untold numbers of military aviators lost their lives grappling with rudimentary aircraft. Even into World War II, training accidents were a never-ending battle for new flyers and their commands. Harmon was no stranger to these accidents or the toll they took on the units and the men who flew. The loss of Clark reinforced the belief that only courageous pilots of great skill and enough luck would survive this period. Military aviation in the 1920s and 1930s was a deadly yet necessary business and flying in overseas or unforgiving environments only exacerbated the risks. Internalizing these truths in 1920, Miff Harmon returned to the United States and began the next chapter of his life.

---

[70] Clark Air Base, Philippines was named in honor of Major Harold M. Clark. Clark was hailed as a hero by the residents of the Hawaiian Islands and became a daily fixture in the local press.

Chapter Four: School Days

> "It, therefore, seems clearly indicated that we should look well forward now in the realm of military aviation education in order that our personnel will be able to efficiently function with the potential air power that is "just around the corner," and that we may develop thru study and analysis the best means of employment of this important factor in the accomplishment and perpetuation of our National Aims."
>
> *Colonel Millard F. Harmon, Jr., June 15, 1939*

On July 1, 1920, the War Department permanently transferred Harmon from the Infantry branch of the Army to the Air Service. Thirty-one years old and with only eight years of service, Harmon had participated in two of the early defining moments of airpower: the Punitive Expedition in Mexico and World War I in Europe. Harmon also commanded the 1st Provisional Wing in Mineola, NY, and France Field in Panama. During this entire time, he made numerous professional acquaintances and personal friendships with people who either were or would become influential in the Army and its air arm, including Hap Arnold, George Marshall, John Pershing, Billy Mitchell, Benjamin Foulois, Carl Spaatz, James Fechet, and Davenport Johnson. Harmon belonged in this group as a decorated, respected, and seasoned combat pilot ready for the continuing challenges of command.

Numerous leadership opportunities and several years of continuing education characterized the next twenty years of Harmon's career. From April 1921 to July the following year, he served on the Advisory Board of the Air Service in Washington, DC. Analogous to the modern commander's action group for the Chief of the Air Service, the Advisory Board represented the best and brightest minds of the Air Service, solving difficult problems for Air Service senior leaders. In July 1922, Harmon and his family moved to Fort Leavenworth, Kansas, to attend the Army's Command and General Staff School. After one year of land-centric studies, Miff taught military science and tactics and was the commander of the Reserve Officer Training Corps (ROTC) detachment at the University of Washington in Seattle. The Army curtailed this tour in August 1924, ordering Harmon to Washington, DC, to attend the Army War College.

While a student at the Army War College, he co-authored a memorandum for the Commandant of the school entitled "Joint Army and Navy Action in Coast Defense." In summary, the paper highlighted the increasing need for cooperation between the services to maximize their effectiveness in future combat operations. Harmon believed it was axiomatic "that in order to wage war effectively, the closest cooperation and the most efficient coordination of effort between the Army and the Navy is essential at all stages of planning and execution."[71]

Harmon leveraged his extensive operational experience and clearly summarized many of the problems he had seen to date with combined actions. Intense coordination was necessary as units

---

[71] Memorandum for: The Assistant Commandant, The Army Way College, "Joint Army and Navy Action in Coast Defense," 23 May 1925, in Personal Papers of Col Harmon, 168.604-17, IRIS No. 00124148, AFHRA.

engaged in modern warfare. Harmon's observations during the Punitive Expedition and World War I paid dividends for his war college paper and later influenced his thinking at the Air Corps Tactical School.

Following his assignment at the Army War College, Harmon served as a member of the G-3 (Operations) division on the War Department staff in Washington, DC. In June 1927, he moved back to California, taking command of the Air Corps Primary Flying School at March Field. As commander of the flight school there, Harmon helped train several aviators who went on to serve in World War II, including most notably Haywood Hansell and Curt LeMay. Harmon returned to Fort Leavenworth, Kansas, in the summer of 1930, where he taught aviation subjects at the Command and General Staff School for two years before again moving, this time to Barksdale Field, Louisiana.

Figure 7: Harmon at Barksdale. Major Harmon, on horseback, and his family at Barksdale Field, LA. Daughter Helen on horseback. Wife Alberta and son 'Buddy' holding their four dogs, Cloudy, Mike, Flyer, and Billy. Source: Photo courtesy of the Eight Air Force Museum, Barksdale AFB, Helen Harmon Nazzaro Collection.

Returning to his permanent grade of Major following the demobilization of World War I, Millard Harmon was the first commander of Barksdale Field on the outskirts of Shreveport, Louisiana, arriving on station in July 1932 and presiding over dedication exercises on February 2, 1933. While at Barksdale, Harmon led an incredible construction and development effort, directing a Herculean effort to transform acres of forest, swamp, and dirt into one of the Air Corps' premier flight stations still in operation today. Shortly after opening the field, numerous flying organizations filled the skies and began calling Barksdale home. Harmon's organizational and leadership skills aside, he also made a lasting impact on the local community. The Shreveport government, businesses, and local citizens all held Miff and his family in high regard. In retrospect, Harmon deserved "much credit for the excellence of the field" during its development, operation, and ultimate expansion.[72]

Harmon left the pursuit world behind and transferred to Luke Field, Hawaii, in December 1936. Taking command of the field and the 5th Bombardment Group was a new challenge for the career fighter pilot. During his tenure as group commander, Harmon put the newest Air Corps bombers, the Douglas B-18 Bolo bomber, through their paces. Harmon also oversaw the development of B-18 tactics and doctrine in spite of a period of constantly changing bombsights and accessory equipment.[73] Because of the numerous changes to aircraft systems, Harmon reported his group was

---

[72] History of Barksdale Field, Courtesy of the 8th Bomb Wing History Office, 7.
[73] Colonel M. F. Harmon, Commander, Luke Field, to Colonel S. W. Fitzgerald, Office, Chief of Staff, letter, 14 July 1938, in Personal Papers of Col Harmon, 168.604-2, IRIS No. 00124141, AFHRA.

behind on bombing effectiveness and inspired his successor to keep training the crews.[74]

In spring of 1938, Harmon led his bombardment group through a series of Army/Navy air and sea exercises. Miff reported his exercise impressions to Hap Arnold, then the assistant chief of the Air Corps in May 1938, focusing predominantly on what he called the "Naval critique." Harmon reported the commanding officer, a naval captain, used the Army air forces ineffectively. In particular, Harmon did not like the commander's tight grip on all operations and failure to utilize junior commanders. He wrote the "commanding officer takes direct control of too much detail," thereby impeding subordinate commanders' ability to make decisions.

In contrast, Harmon felt that Air Corps commanders understood their mission and operated within the boundaries of sound doctrine and common sense, whereas in the exercise, junior commanders were prevented from doing so. Harmon also commented on the Navy's undermanned staff organizations and their failure to disseminate valuable intelligence in time-critical situations.[75] Harmon's critique of this exercise identified serious issues facing the services during the interwar period. Short on manpower and resources, the Army and Navy struggled to maintain their core competencies while ignoring opportunities for joint integration. Additionally, Harmon warned Arnold about the necessity for competent staff agencies during crises. Harmon witnessed ineffective staff organizations while in France during World War I and again saw a lack of attention to detail necessary for successful combat operations. Harmon's emphasis on

---

[74] Harmon to Fitzgerald, 14 July 1938.
[75] Harmon to Arnold, 7 May 1938, 1-2.

competent staff work was a very mature yet remotely held belief in the flying-centric world of the Air Corps.

The War Department curtailed Harmon's assignment in Hawaii to send him stateside again. Reflecting on his command tenure in a letter to his troops before leaving, Harmon congratulated his men for a job well done. He highlighted the notable achievements accomplished by his group, including 17,000 flight hours, multiple joint exercises, and the development of new air tactics, all without an accident.[76]

Time in Hawaii imparted to Harmon valuable joint perspectives. While there, he learned again that the Army and Navy are considerably different organizations with dissimilar modes of operation. Then as now, the manners in which officers from different services command their personnel and design their operations are reflections of their specific service cultures. Harmon advocated the centralized command and decentralized execution of operations orders, placing great trust in the members of his command. These lessons learned in peacetime were situations Harmon would see in wartime when he returned to the Pacific during World War II.

Molding the Air Corps Tactical School

On July 18, 1938, a mildly disappointed Harmon relinquished command of Luke Field, Honolulu, and proceeded via ocean liner and train to Maxwell Field, Alabama, and the Air Corps Tactical School (ACTS), where he assumed the post of Assistant Commandant. The assignment to the Air Corps' center of strategic

---

[76] General Orders, Luke Field, by Colonel Millard F. Harmon, Jr., 15 July 1938 with handwritten corrections, in Personal papers of Col Harmon, 1920-1938, 168.604-11, IRIS No. 00124144, AFHRA.

thought surprised Harmon, who, in a letter to Major General Oscar Westover, Chief of the Air Corps, said that he "never particularly fancied [himself] as a high powered 'school fellow.'"[77] Yet by then, Harmon was a vocal and highly regarded officer in matters of airpower thought. Two years earlier, for instance, while he commanded Barksdale Field, the ACTS distributed its cornerstone document, "Air Force," for comments. The 3rd Air Force commander appointed Lieutenant Colonel Harmon, president of a board of five officers, to review the text and submit proposed changes. In a four-page, single-spaced, typed response, Harmon offered detailed and critical thoughts on all sections of the Air Corps text. The document reflected the predominant airpower theories of the mid-1930s. By then, the concepts of High Altitude Precision Daylight Bombing and the limited efficacy of pursuit aviation had firmly entrenched themselves among ACTS instructors.[78] "By 1933, instruction in the employment of the air forces centered on the interdependence of the segments of the economic structure of a nation," all of which could be brought under attack by bombers.[79] The introduction of the XB-17 bomber in 1935 only intensified matters at ACTS, which in turn produced the document under consideration by Harmon and his board of officers.[80]

Throughout Harmon's review of the "Air Force" text, he criticized the difficult manner in which it was written, questioning

[77] Colonel M.F. Harmon, Commander, Luke Field, to Major General O. Westover, Chief of the Air Corps, letter 30 June 1938, in Personal papers of Col Harmon, 1920-1938, 168.604-11, IRIS No. 00124141, AFHRA.
[78] Robert T. Finney, *History of the Air Corps Tactical School, 1920-1940*, USAF Historical Study 100 (Maxwell AFB, AL: USAF Historical Division, Air University, 1955), 31.
[79] Finney, *History of the Air Corps Tactical School*, 32.
[80] Finney, *History of the Air Corps Tactical School*, 33.

whether "any student's conception of air power would be improved by such a technical and complex definition is doubtful."[81] Furthermore, he rebuked the notion of "exactitudes" and called into question the "certain doctrines which the text accepts apparently without reservation."[82] In particular, Harmon was not pleased with the lack of consideration given to the human elements required to maintain and employ air forces successfully. The text stated that "the powers and limitations of an air force are determined by the characteristics of its equipment (airplanes) and that personnel is, therefore, inferior in importance."[83] Harmon's personal experiences in the Punitive Expedition and World War I flew in direct opposition to these notions. Harmon responded that "this attitude appears to ignore the fact that any equipment is useful only in so far as it is efficiently maintained and effectively employed by skilled personnel."[84] This fact would become readily evident in the South Pacific campaign of 1942.

In another section of the prepared critique, Harmon called into question the ACTS assertion that base selection can mitigate the effects of weather. The "Air Force" document argued, "adequate bases will prevent air forces from being affected by weather 'to any greater extent than any other forces.'"[85] Harmon responded by stating that "it is difficult to understand how adequate bases are to

---

[81] Brigadier General G.C. Brant, Commander, Third Wing, to Commanding General, General Headquarters Air Force, memorandum, "Criticism of Air Corps Tactical School Text 'Air Force,'" 14 March 1936, with appendices 1 & 2, in Personal papers of Col Harmon, 1920-1938, 248.126-4, AFHRA. (Hereafter cited as "Brant to COMGEN, GHAF").
[82] Brant to COMGEN, GHAF, appendix 2.
[83] Brant to COMGEN, GHAF, appendix 2, author's emphasis.
[84] Brant to COMGEN, GHAF, appendix 2.
[85] Brant to COMGEN, GHAF, appendix 2.

make flying in bad weather any less difficult."[86] The ACTS text further downplayed the role of logistics and maintenance of air forces during warfare, to which Harmon replied, "surely, an air force, like any other force, can be defeated by stopping its supplies and replacements, and it might be hopelessly crippled by air combat or anti-aircraft."[87] Therefore, he proposed that "certain important limitations of an Air Force should be given more consideration. Serious limitations not mentioned include: the necessity for frequent returns to base for fuel and ammunition; inability to operate efficiently without prepared airdromes; inability to operate under certain weather conditions."[88]

Harmon's response reflected years of combat and command experience. Moreover, it served as a premonition of his time in the South Pacific during World War II. Harmon's attempt to punctuate the Air Corps' foundational document with real-world experience and combat sanity culminated in his final critique of the document, a point that also set him apart from other airpower enthusiasts of the time. In response to the ACTS assertion that "there is no counterpart of the battle in air warfare," Harmon simply wrote that this belief "may not always be true."[89] Harmon emphasized that most of the ACTS document relied on unproven theories delivered as factual analysis. He wrote, "a note of caution should be sounded against the too ardent adoption of peacetime theories and hypothesis when they are not supported by actually demonstrated facts nor by the experiences of the only war in which aviation was employed."[90]

---

[86] Brant to COMGEN, GHAF, appendix 2.
[87] Brant to COMGEN, GHAF, appendix 2.
[88] Brant to COMGEN, GHAF, appendix 2.
[89] Brant to COMGEN, GHAF, appendix 2.
[90] Brant to COMGEN, GHAF, appendix 1.

Changing the Rules

Now the Assistant Commandant of the ACTS, Harmon found himself in a position to influence thinking at the Air Corps' premier school. Almost immediately after settling in at Maxwell, Harmon set about incorporating a more balanced airpower course of instruction, integrating air and surface force curricula, and increasing student enrollment in anticipation of a future war.

Further proof of Harmon's reputation as a critical thinker is evident in a letter from Claire Chennault written on July 28, 1939 when Chennault, then engaged in the support of Chinese forces against the Japanese, wrote Harmon to be considered an instructor at ACTS. Chennault respected Harmon as a pursuit pioneer and offered to share his own recent experiences in China if Harmon felt his "observations would be of some value" to the officers at the ACTS.[91]

In fact, pursuit instruction at ACTS was on a slow road to recovery when Miff arrived as the Assistant Commandant. After reaching "its all-time low during the period 1934 to 1936," Harmon set out to give pursuit subjects at ACTS renewed emphasis.[92] Outlining his beliefs on pursuit instruction to Brigadier General Barton Yount, the Assistant Chief of the Air Corps, Harmon explained that his initial finding at ACTS was the pursuit "pendulum

---

[91] C. L. Chennault, American Consul, Kunming, China, to Colonel M.F. Harmon, Assistant Commandant, Air Corps Tactical School, letter, 28 July 1939, in Personal Collection of Millard F. Harmon, 168.604-13, IRIS No. 00124144, AFHRA.

[92] Colonel M.F. Harmon, Assistant Commandant, Air Corps Tactical School, to Brigadier General B.K. Yount, letter, 25 November 1939, Personal papers of Col Harmon, AFHRA.

had started its swing back to a position of well-reasoned normalcy."[93]

Figure 8: Harmon at Maxwell. Colonel Harmon's official photo as the Assistant Commandant of the Air Corps Tactical School, Maxwell Field, Alabama. Source: Millard F. Harmon, III. Picture in author's personal collection.

Although Harmon was predominantly a pursuit pilot by trade, he had spent eighteen months in the 5th Bombardment Group and lobbied for increased bombardment capabilities. With this in mind, Harmon advocated a balanced approach toward airpower instruction and wrote, "pursuit and bombardment are both essentials."[94] He believed "they are not interchangeable in their

[93] Harmon to Yount, 25 November 1939.
[94] Harmon to Yount, 25 November 1939.

principal roles...hence that there were no ordained proportion[s] between the two."[95]

Harmon tackled other syllabus revisions as the Assistant Commandant. During the spring of 1939, the Air Corps staff recognized several inadequacies of aviation instruction at basic Army schools. Designed primarily to instruct future ground commanders, the core Army schooling was failing to adjust to the changing nature of air warfare, and as a result, the Air Corps convened a board of officers in Washington, DC, to discuss the way forward. Their directive was to make "recommendations for changes in the Air Corps course of instruction at the Command and General Staff School."[96] The board of three officers included Brigadier General Barton Yount, the Chief of the Air Corps, Colonel Lewis Brereton, an instructor at the Army Command and General Staff School at Fort Leavenworth, Kansas, and Harmon.

The initial discussion immediately focused on the "wide appreciation of the fact that there is a growing necessity for a broader and more intimate knowledge by all officers of the Army concerning the employment of [the] Air Force."[97] The board's goal was to expose more officers, especially quality officers attending the Command and General Staff School, to the fundamental aviation principles that would enable them to utilize airpower in the future. To accomplish this goal, the board made a major recommendation to increase the time allotted to Air Corps studies at the school from forty to sixty hours during the 1939-1940

---

[95] Harmon to Yount, 25 November 1939.
[96] Proceedings of a board of officers convened in the Office, Chief of the Air Corps, Washington, DC, 19 April 1939, 245-04B, IRIS No. 00155793, in Millard F. Harmon, Jr. Papers, AFHRA, 2. (Hereafter cited as "Proceedings").
[97] Proceedings, 2.

academic years.[98] The board identified additional courses for instruction, including the 'Air Estimate of the Situation,' 'Application of Air Power to National Strategic Problems,' 'The Strategic Air Offensive,' 'The Ultimate Objective,' and the 'Influence of Air Bases on Air Operations.'[99] Still, the board felt that five more hours were required and offered to add courses in 'Joint Action of the Air Force with the Navy,' regarding the coastal defense of the United States, and 'Air Force Tactical Offensive and Defensive' to the 1940-1941 syllabus.[100] In a handwritten note at the bottom of the board proceedings, Harmon indicated that in mid-1939, the Leavenworth syllabus added twenty-two hours and an entirely new course titled 'Air Force Tactical Offensive and Defensive.'[101]

A Complete Overhaul

A couple of months later, Harmon went further than the board and proposed a total revision to the educational path for Air Corps officers, not simply syllabus refinements at a few schools. He believed the intellectual demands of flying, coupled with the rapid advances in technology and tactics, required Air Corps officers to attend more schooling than provided by the basic Army courses such as the Command and General Staff School. To this end, Harmon authored a monograph entitled the "Policy for Future Military Education of Air Corps Officers" and coordinated his ideas with fellow officers. Harmon clearly stated his principal concerns in the opening paragraphs. "The general military educational system

[98] Proceedings, 3.
[99] Proceedings, 4.
[100] Proceedings, 5.
[101] Proceedings, 1. Handwritten notes initialed 'MFH' at the bottom of the coversheet.

of the Army was not designed particularly with the Air Corps in mind," he wrote.[102] "In brief, the Air Corps schools have been 'fitted into' the established system. The major position now held and in the future to be maintained by the Air Corps in National Defense is tantamount in importance to that now held by the 'ground' Army and the Navy and the evolvement of a suitable and adequate system for the military education of Air Corps personnel becomes daily of more importance."[103]

Harmon further believed the Air Corps would achieve a "parity with the Army and the Navy in the scheme of National Defense or absorb them one or both."[104] Miff believed technological advancements in the field of airpower would outpace the development of land or naval forces. He stated aviation progress

---

[102] Proceedings, 4.

[103] "Policy for Future Military Education of Air Corps Officers, Preliminary Rough Draft," by Millard F. Harmon, Jr., 15 June 1939, 245-04B, IRIS No. 00155793, in Millard F. Harmon, Jr. Papers, AFHRA, 2.

[104] Harmon, Policy for Future Military Education of Air Corps Officers, 3, author's emphasis. (Hereafter cited as "Policy for Future PME"). Note: LtCol Peter R. Faber, (author of "*Interwar US Army Aviation and the Air Corps Tactical School: Incubators of American Airpower*," in *The Paths of Heaven: The Evolution of Airpower Theory*, ed. Col Phillip S. Meilinger, Air University Press, 1997, page 198), references this paragraph but states "Harmon, however, could not decide if the long-range bomber would 'assume parity with the Army and Navy...or absorb them one or both.'" I believe this to be an incorrect representation of Harmon's position. Nowhere in Harmon's monograph does he mention long-range bombers, and, it is widely known that while Harmon was familiar with Air Corps bombing doctrine and flew bombers himself for a short period, Harmon was, by all definition a pursuit pilot. Moreover, Harmon was a balanced airpower theorist giving each theory its due regard (see Harmon to Yount, November 25, 1939, AFHRA, where Harmon states that the "Bombardment invincibility doctrine which reached it culmination a few years ago, with its consequent influence on Pursuit prestige irked me no end.") In sum, I do not believe Harmon would ever hold long-range bombing could supplant either the Army or Navy, rather, he advocated the rise of an independent Air Corps that would achieve parity with the other services.

would be measured in years compared to "quarter-centuries as with the development of navies."[105] He further believed Air Corps officers must "look well forward" regarding the educational syllabus for airmen to remain prepared for the ever-changing aviation environment.[106] Similar to the quandary faced in today's Air Force, where the development of space, cyberspace, manned and unmanned systems often outpace the development of tactics or doctrine, Harmon argued airmen were required to look well outside of present operating procedures to consider what may be beyond the horizon.

To stay abreast of the evolving field of aviation studies, Harmon proposed a variety of schools selectively positioned throughout the career of the Air Corps officer. Following initial training at the Air Corps Training Center, he advocated the assignment of junior officers to tactical units again to polish their basic combat training. Junior officers would concentrate on the "tactics and techniques of subordinate units," develop, and 'fix' their flying ability.[107] Upon successful completion of this tactical assignment and if selected for advancement, officers would then attend a one-year Air Corps Technical School with a return to tactical units for a period of two years.

At this point in an officer's development, Harmon advocated both the officer and the Air Corps staff make a career decision. The majority of Air Corps officers would proceed down the traditional line-officer career consisting of service with tactical units, schools, and military staff work. A smaller group of officers would pursue more technical career paths such as engineering, research and

[105] Harmon, Policy for Future PME, 3.
[106] Harmon, Policy for Future PME, 3.
[107] Harmon, Policy for Future PME, 4.

development, meteorology, or communications. Line officers would attend the Basic or Squadron Officer Course offered at the Air Corps Tactical School. The Basic Course would be "designed to qualify junior officers for the discharge of all duties involving group staff, squadron command, and staff and joint operations of minor units."[108]

Staff work was a requirement in Harmon's view, and proper schooling was necessary to ensure Air Corps officers were prepared to execute the staff's mission. Experience in World War I showed that schools established for every major element of warfighting, including military staffing, were "essential for the successful prosecution of the battle mission."[109] Upon successful completion of this one-year school, junior officers would return to tactical units for approximately four to six more years. Officers selected for careers that were more technical would attend schools such as the Air Corps Engineering School, Aeronautical Engineering and Meteorology at California or Houston Tech, Harvard School of Business Administration, and others.[110]

Following a five-year tactical tour, line officers would return to the Air Corps Tactical School and participate in the Advanced Course. The Advanced Course would concentrate on large unit logistics, joint planning and operations with field armies and naval forces, establishment and organization of air bases, higher echelon command and staff procedures, and finally, "strategic studies designed to develop practical plans for countering or neutralizing

---

[108] Harmon, Policy for Future PME, 6.
[109] Colonel M.F. Harmon, Assistant Commandant, Air Corps Tactical School, to Major General H.H. Arnold, Chief of the Air Corps, letter, 9 October 1939, in Personal Collection of Millard F. Harmon, 168.604-12, IRIS No. 00124143, AFHRA.
[110] Harmon, Policy for Future PME, 5.

any major threat against [the] National policies."[111] Graduates of the ACTS Advanced Course would be thoroughly familiar with the most current Air Corps policies, procedures, and doctrine. From this position of intellectual potency and following a general assignment as school instructors or Corps Area liaison officers with other services, graduates would attend the Army or Navy War Colleges. While attending those major military schools, ACTS graduates would finalize their professional education and be prepared to communicate effectively about the appropriate application of airpower.[112]

The Air Corps staff gave Colonel Harmon's educational proposals glowing marks. Reporting from the office of the Chief of the Air Corps, Lieutenant Colonel George Stratemeyer wrote Harmon that he found Harmon's monograph to be "exceptionally interesting" and conveyed that both Yount and Arnold were in agreement with him.[113] In a summation of a letter from Yount endorsed by Arnold, Stratemeyer quoted Yount, who said Harmon's monograph was "a step in the right direction."[114] Because of Harmon's beliefs, Yount further proposed to establish a new board of officers to review and consider an overhaul of the Air Corps educational system in line with Harmon's suggestions.

By late 1939 and early 1940, Harmon's ideas and the work done by the education board had garnered much attention in the Air Corps and Army writ large. General George Marshall, Chief of Staff

---

[111] Harmon, Policy for Future PME, 6.
[112] Harmon, Policy for Future PME, 5.
[113] Lieutenant Colonel G.E. Stratemeyer, Office of the Chief of the Air Corps, to Colonel M.F. Harmon, Assistant Commandant, Air Corps Tactical School, letter, 22 July 1939, in Personal Collection of Millard F. Harmon, 245-04B, IRIS No. 00155793, AFHRA.
[114] Stratemeyer to Harmon, 22 July 1939.

of the War Department, visited Maxwell in January 1940, just prior to the board of officers meeting to redesign the Air Corps' educational system. Although Marshall's visit was "unexpected and ...hurried," he found the conversations with ACTS instructors to be highly profitable and most certainly listened to Colonel Harmon, whom he had now known for over twenty years.[115] In light of the meeting, Marshall asked Harmon to write him a frank "estimate of the situation."[116]

Although it is unclear what General Marshall discussed with the ACTS instructors, Harmon's response to him indicates he may have been concerned with the course duration and the limited amount of time spent discussing land warfare concepts. In response to Marshall's request, it appears Harmon prepared at least two letters: the first is a draft dated January 30, 1940 with Harmon's handwritten note stating "not used," and the second, a day later, prepared by Harmon and Muir S. Fairchild, an instructor at ACTS. It is important to delineate the two documents because the messages are different, shedding light possibly on what Marshall desired and the manner in which the ACTS faculty chose to answer him. The first draft memo and the second draft memo address course-length questions adequately. The long and short courses at ACTS strove to cover the same material, while the short course condensed many practical exercises into a few. The Air Corps built the short course to expose rapidly more officers to the ACTS teachings during the turbulent period leading up to World War II.

---

[115] General G.C. Marshall, Chief of Staff, War Department, to Colonel M.F. Harmon, Assistant Commandant, Air Corps Tactical School, letter, 26 January 1940, in Personal Collection of Millard F. Harmon, 245-04B, IRIS No. 00155793, AFHRA.

[116] Marshall to Harmon, 26 January 1940.

The major differences between the "memo' are apparent in their treatment of the amount of time dedicated to the study of land warfare concepts. The first draft memo is bold, stating many of the concepts taught at ACTS were theories untested in war situations. Additionally, the first memo advocates a more aggressive use of the neighboring infantry school to conduct combined arms exercises similar to the ACTS-Infantry School exercise that occurred in early February 1940. It appears Marshall advocated more time devoted within the ACTS syllabus to combined arms exercises. "Perhaps," Harmon wrote in his first draft, "we have not made a proper evaluation, and acting upon your suggestion, the present class with have double the time" to witness demonstrations at the Infantry School.[117] Furthermore, Harmon advocated, "consideration should be given to a maximum use of the adjacent facilities of the Infantry School in order to supplement academic presentation with practical demonstrations."[118]

In his second draft, Harmon reduced the amount of discussion regarding combined arms exercises and the necessity to interact with the Infantry School. Instead of advocating more exercises, Harmon defended the amount contained in the syllabus, stating Air Corps students who participate in such events will gain a "clear understanding of the tactical functioning of the other branches."[119]

---

[117] Colonel M.F. Harmon, Assistant Commandant, Air Corps Tactical School, to General G.C. Marshall, Chief of Staff, War Department, draft letter, 30 January 1940, in Personal Collection of Millard F. Harmon, 248.126, IRIS No. 00157788, AFHRA, 4.

[118] Harmon to Marshall, 30 January 1940, 5.

[119] Colonel M.F. Harmon, Assistant Commandant, Air Corps Tactical School, to General G.C. Marshall, Chief of Staff, War Department, draft letter #2, n.d., in Personal Collection of Millard F. Harmon, 248.126, IRIS No. 00157788, AFHRA, 5.

In other words, Harmon felt the current amount of emphasis placed on combined exercises was both necessary and sufficient.

Fear of Change at the ACTS

It was in this context that Harmon coordinated air and infantry exercises with the Infantry School in nearby Fort Benning, Georgia. Previously, on January 31, 1940, Colonel Harmon orchestrated a large combined arms exercise between Air Corps Tactical School officers and students attending the Infantry School. Harmon's experiences supporting infantry operations in Mexico taught him the value of pre-mission planning and close coordination with infantry units. To this end, Harmon initiated a practical flying exercise where ACTS students participated in division maneuvers and acted as forward airborne observers and reconnaissance pilots.

In preparation for the exercise, the school provided students with a map of the training area, a brief overview of the expected division maneuvers, and specific requests for information they were to gather. Safety precluded more than six aircraft in the area at one time, and most of the machines were trainer aircraft, thus unsuitable for observation work. Additionally, no students were familiar with the local flying area, and few students had previous practical observation experience. Despite these limitations, all students gained an appreciation for several key elements that determined the success or failure of a military observation mission.

First, students learned that pre-mission planning was critical. This included map study, pilot-observer crew coordination, and most significantly, the "importance of training and experience in cooperation with ground troops in order to accomplish successfully such a mission."[120] Second, ACTS students saw first-hand the "rapidity [with] which a ground situation can change when motorized units [were] involved."[121] The technological advancements in mechanized warfare had changed since World War I, and across forgiving terrain, the pace of land warfare was rapidly accelerating. While students during this period read of the overwhelming success of Blitzkrieg-style warfare and the invasion of Poland only a few months prior, the first-hand experience gained in this practical exercise was invaluable. After completion of the practical exercises, Harmon wrote a letter to the Assistant Commandant of the Infantry School, Brigadier General Courtney Hodges, later to become full General and a decorated officer for actions in Europe during World War II. Harmon wrote that the exercise overall was a success, and several critical lessons were learned by the ACTS students and faculty.

This exercise was not without its opponents, however. In an appreciative letter to General Hodges, Major General Hap Arnold, then Chief of the Air Corps, wrote that the "plans, as worked out by you and Harmon, appear to be excellent, and should greatly improve the instruction at the [Air Corps] Tactical School."[122] He further wrote that he was "anxious to take advantage of the facilities [at the Infantry School]."[123] However, in a separate note

---

[120] Colonel M.F. Harmon, Assistant Commandant, Air Corps Tactical School, to Colonel C.H. Hodges, Assistant Commandant, The Infantry School, letter, 2 February 1940, in Personal Collection of Millard F. Harmon, 168.604-11A, IRIS No. 00124142, AFHRA.
[121] Harmon to Hodges, 2 February 1940.
[122] Major General H.H. Arnold, Chief of the Air Corps, to Colonel C.H. Hodges, Assistant Commandant, The Infantry School, letter, 30 January 1940, in Personal Collection of Millard F. Harmon, 168.604-11A, IRIS No. 00124142, AFHRA.
[123] Arnold to Hodges, 30 January 1940.

dated one day later, Arnold cautioned Harmon about the changes he was making at ACTS. Arnold told Harmon to "use [his] own judgment bearing in mind at all times that [the Air Corps is] now condensing into three months what has previously required one year to properly instruct personnel passing through [his] hands."[124]

He further warned Harmon not to allow him to "be railroaded into changing it from an air to a ground school."[125] Harmon responded to Arnold, saying his "remark concerning the maintenance of the air character of this School will be given full value."[126] Harmon also wrote, "no increase in the total time now allocated to ground arms will be made," rather, more instruction can be given by streamlining the academic processes at ACTS.[127]

Although Harmon served in the Assistant Commandant capacity for only two years, he made vast changes to the professional education system for Air Corps officers. A graduate of the Army War College and a graduate and instructor at the Command and General Staff School, Harmon was intimately familiar with these courses and the inadequacies of those syllabi regarding the effective employment of airpower. Harmon's proposed revision to the Air Corps educational system is reflected in the professional military education system in the United States Air Force today. Additionally, he advocated a hands-on approach to

---

[124] Major General H.H. Arnold, Chief of the Air Corps, to Colonel M.F. Harmon, Assistant Commandant, Air Corps Tactical School, letter, 1 February 1940, in Personal Collection of Millard F. Harmon, 168.604-11A, IRIS No. 00124142, AFHRA.

[125] Arnold to Harmon, 1 Feb 1940, author's emphasis.

[126] Colonel M.F. Harmon, Assistant Commandant, Air Corps Tactical School, to Major General H.H. Arnold, Chief of the Air Corps, letter, 5 February 1940, in Personal Collection of Millard F. Harmon, 168.604-11A, IRIS No. 00124142, AFHRA.

[127] Harmon to Arnold, 5 February 1940.

many difficult subjects, such as observation, combined arms employment, and map exercises.

His efforts to join forces with the Infantry School were a reflection of his own personal difficulties experienced in the deserts of Mexico or over the trench lines in France. This background taught him that coordination with ground units was critical on the modern battlefield. The pace of maneuver warfare and the dynamic nature of the modern enemy meant that supporting airpower and land units required frequent and detailed interaction to ensure success. Timely and accurate intelligence, careful map study, thorough crew coordination, and knowledge of the scheme of maneuver were some of the lessons learned during the combined exercises with the Infantry School. Harmon's efforts exposed many ACTS students to these challenges. During this same time, Harmon labored to implement a modern ACTS syllabus rich with experience and real-world knowledge. The move away from 'bomber invincibility' to a more balanced aviation approach, with an appreciation for logistics, weather, and enemy reactions, were welcome additions to an officer corps preparing to fight the greatest war in history. All the while, it is clear that the struggle for an independent Air Force was first and foremost of the mind of Hap Arnold. Cautioning Harmon to preserve the "air character" of the school despite pressures from senior Army commanders, served as a premonition of future inter War Department struggles that would manifest during World War II. A war that was finally nearing the doorsteps of the United States.

On June 13, 1940, the Chief of the Air Corps suspended instruction at ACTS, and Harmon left for his next assignment in nearby Texas.[128] However, in those two short years at Maxwell,

[128] Finney, *History of the Air Corps Tactical School*, 41.

Colonel Harmon left his legacy on the students and instructors who served with him. Those that passed through the halls of the ACTS during Harmon's time are on the honor roll of leaders during World War II and beyond. Men like Curt LeMay, Glen Jamison, Walter Weaver, Donald Wilson, Earle Partridge, Laurence Kuter, Muir Fairchild, Lauris Norstad, James Andersen, and others studied under the system Miff Harmon built.[129]

---

[129] Finney, *History of the Air Corps Tactical School*, 60 – 63, 76 – 86.

Chapter Five: Witness to 'The Blitz'

> "War is an Air war today. The Air alone can bring Germany to its knees if anything can. The Navy can only ensure the existence of England, the Air can bring the war home to Central Germany and break down morale."
>
> *Henry H. "Hap" Arnold, England, April 21, 1941*

The year 1940 was a watershed event for the Army Air Forces in the United States. After watching the speed and destructive power of military air forces in Europe, the War Department began a vast expansion of personnel, equipment, and airfields throughout the nation. As the new commanding officer of the Gulf Coast Air Corps Training Center, headquartered at Randolph Field, Texas, Harmon confronted this growth directly. Upon taking command, the War Department told Harmon to meet the "requirements of an expansion program being undertaken to produce upwards to 7,000 officer-pilots a year."[130] Within only a few months, the Training Center was well on its way to achieving that goal. Subsequently, the Army promoted Harmon to Brigadier General and immediately gave him a new command in California.

Growth in the nation's air arm meant vast expansion of the air bases and air commands around the United States. One particular

---

[130] *Form One*, Vol 1, No. 4, Sept 1940, Miscellaneous Correspondence of General Millard F. Harmon, Millard F. Harmon Papers, 168-604.13, IRIS No. 00124144, AFHRA, 18.

field that became strategically important was Hamilton Field in Marin County, California. Located just a few miles north of San Rafael, Hamilton Field had recently converted from a bomber base to a fighter base, and its first commander as a fighter field was Miff Harmon. On November 22, 1940, Harmon became Commanding General of Hamilton Field and immediately began to oversee the rapid growth at this base. Hamilton Field, surrounded by major industrial manufacturing interests in the Bay Area, and centrally located on the West Coast of the United States, had as its central goal the defense of these vital areas.[131]

Two months later, on January 16, 1941, the Air Force added to the responsibility on Harmon's shoulders by naming him commander of the 10th Pursuit Wing at Hamilton Field. The very next day, Hap Arnold gave Harmon an even greater assignment. Under secret orders issued by the War Department, Harmon left immediately for the European Theater of war.[132] Upon arrival in England, Brigadier General Miff Harmon's orders were to observe the ongoing military activities and report his findings through the War Department G-2 (Intelligence) section in Washington, DC. Similar to the responsibilities during his 1917 mission to France, Miff served as a Military Observer in England and later as a special Air Advisor to Mr. W. Averell Harriman, President Franklin Roosevelt's Special Minister for war supplies to Great Britain. Major General Arnold, as the Acting Deputy Chief of Staff of the War Department, wrote Harmon in March 1941 and outlined Miff's specific duties. In particular, Arnold wanted Harmon to accomplish two things; first, "get to places and see things that you may not

---

[131] History of Hamilton Field Air Base Area, Feb 1929 – Mar 1944, in the USAF Collection, 284.04-1, IRIS No. 00172978, AFHRA.
[132] History of Hamilton Field Air Base Area, Feb 1929 – Mar 1944, AFHRA.

[know]," and second, "enable Harriman to get reliable information and advice on aviation matters."[133] Harmon was serving two masters from March until June 1941 while in England: the War Department G-2 Intelligence Division with direct lines to Arnold and Marshall and the Harriman Mission with direct ties to President Roosevelt. All while under intense attack by the Luftwaffe.

'The Blitz' over England during World War II was a period of sustained bombing of the UK by Nazi Germany between September 7, 1940 and May 10, 1941. 'The Blitz' was the first major campaign of the war conducted entirely by air forces, and it was the longest and most destructive bombing campaign in history. During this time, the German Luftwaffe launched more than 40,000 air attacks against targets in the UK, killing over 43,000 people and destroying millions of homes. The raids designed to disrupt the British war effort and to demoralize the civilian population, targeted industrial and military sites, as well as civilian areas. The raids were conducted at night, when the British air defenses were weakest, and the Luftwaffe was able to inflict significant damage.

When Harmon arrived in England during the winter of 1941, he noted immediately the bleak circumstances. In a detailed chronological diary, Harmon kept notes on all meetings, observations, and even dinner parties. Like his World War I diary of events in France, Harmon's sharp perceptions and blunt reporting make for great historical reading. Harmon's accounts of the daily German raids on England during 'The Blitz' are gripping. He witnessed dozens of dogfights from the ground and experienced

---

[133] Lieutenant General H.H. Arnold, Chief of Air Corps, to Major General M.F. Harmon, Chief of Staff, Chief of Air Corps, letter, 10 March 1941, in Miscellaneous Correspondence and Related Material, 1936-1945, in Millard F. Harmon Papers, 168-604.13, IRIS No. 00124144, AFHRA.

the Luftwaffe bombing efforts firsthand. On April 17, 1941, Harmon recorded one of the worst attacks on London.

"Last night London was subjected to the most severe air raid of the war so far. It is estimated that approx. 300 bombers participated, and the destruction was terrific and widespread. I watched it from the beginning to the end from the west – S – west windows of my room at the Dorchester – overlooking Park Lane and Hyde Park, from about 4/16/41 – 2200 to 4/17/41 – 0420. The attack was concentrated at first along the strand with H. E.[134] Bombs and evidently oil bombs as three large fires were quickly started.

"The whining fall of bombs was not particularly pleasing, especially when they came quite close, as several did – bursting just across Park Lane from the Dorchester, rocking the building and throwing dirt and junk all over it. However, they sounded closer than they actually were. I should judge that the closest was some 50 yds. away and I was certain that it was going to hit my room.

"Subsequent reports indicate that there were between 400 and 450 individual airplane (Bomber) attacks that night on London. Judged by the weight of attack, material damage done and casualties it is definitely stated to have been the most severe of the war."[135]

Besides the daily reporting of ongoing combat activities, it is apparent that Miff Harmon was pleased with the British air war effort. Harmon toured all major air commands, Royal Air Force (RAF) military headquarters, and numerous bases in England. In

---

[134] High-explosive

[135] Diary of General Harmon for Mrs. Harmon – 1941, 18 Jan 1941 – 31 Mar 41, Book No. 2, in Millard F. Harmon Papers, 168.604-46, IRIS No. 00124170, AFHRA. (Hereafter cited as "Harmon Diary in England").

addition, he met with and discussed war efforts with the great British air leaders of the day: Air Chief Marshal Charles Portal, Chief of the RAF Air Staff, Air Marshal Arthur Harris, Commander in Chief of Bomber Command, Air Chief Marshal Sir Hugh Dowding, Air Vice Marshal Trafford Lee-Mallory, Commander of 12th Group and Air Vice Marshal William Sholto Douglas, Commander in Chief of Fighter Command. Harmon's initial impressions of English doctrine were favorable and compared well to American ideas. As the recent Assistant Commandant of the Air Corps Tactical School, Harmon assessed "no outstanding doctrines of tactics that are dissimilar to our own or better than our conceptions."[136] Harmon also commented favorably on the British linkage between strategic policy and operational means. On February 12, 1941, Harmon wrote the "strategic plan formulated by Air Ministry and, subject to that, C in C Bomb Comd. has 'free rein.'"[137]

Visions of the South Pacific

Harmon's notes contain detailed investigative efforts he made into pursuit basing, capabilities, tactics, and effectiveness against the Luftwaffe. In multiple entries throughout Harmon's diary, he comments on a variety of factors that later proved to be crucial in his assignment to the South Pacific. First, Harmon noted the need for improved airdromes with concrete runways. In three simple sentences, Harmon wrote, "Runways are real necessity. Had hard time without. Now mostly have."[138] Following one of his multiple visits to airdromes throughout England, Harmon saw that "universally runways are considered essential unless the [existing

---

[136] Harmon Diary in England, 34.
[137] Harmon Diary in England, 9.
[138] Harmon Diary in England, 18.

natural] surface is exceptionally adapted."[139] This realization would haunt Harmon in less than eighteen months when he would command forces in the South Pacific foraging for suitable airdromes areas. Unlike the British fields defended by army personnel and concentrating efforts against air attacks, Harmon's fields in the Solomons would have to defend against Japanese air, ground, and sea assaults every moment of the day.

Second, Harmon immediately recognized the extreme demands placed on pursuit and bomber crews during the months of pitched combat. He identified "no relief or multiple crews" from which a surge could be mustered in an attempt to thwart a German invasion of England.[140] Training of new crews was time-consuming, while experienced aircrews suffered from attrition and the constant stress of combat. While in flight, especially in bomber aircraft at higher altitudes, Harmon noted that interior working conditions wreaked havoc on the aviators. Similar to his experiences over the cold Mexican mountain ranges in 1916, RAF bomber crews dealt with freezing temperatures and deafening engine noises. On board RAF Wellington bombers, the "rear gunner [used] electrically heated clothing" and was kept awake through intermittent conversations with fellow crewmates.[141] Harmon emphasized the need to find solutions to these problems or face even higher attrition of the irreplaceable aircrews.

Third, Harmon observed the changing nature of aerial combat and the requirement to possess pursuit aircraft with adequate capabilities to match the enemy. Prior to World War II, bombers routinely outperformed pursuit fighters, which were restricted to

---

[139] Harmon Diary in England, 31 – 32.

[140] Harmon Diary in England, 8.

[141] Harmon Diary in England, 24.

low and medium altitudes. By 1941, the rapid technological changes in aircraft metallurgy, propulsion, and armament meant that dogfights were regularly occurring at altitudes greater than 17,000 feet and sometimes as high as 32,000 feet in unpressurized cockpits.[142] Harmon noted the need for increased firepower in American fighter aircraft after test-firing a British Supermarine Spitfire. Armored engine compartments, bulletproof windshields, increased rates of fire, and the ability to maneuver at high altitudes were necessary to compete in the air over Europe.[143] In just a few short months, Harmon would see these problems arise firsthand as superior Japanese Zero aircraft easily outclassed his makeshift air force based at Guadalcanal.

Harmon also noted critical shortcomings of the British war effort, especially the 'vast' geographic separation between headquarters and subordinate units. A firm believer that commanders should remain close to their troops, Harmon observed that certain headquarters were too far from their outlying combat squadrons. He noted specific headquarters functions remained distant "because of presumed necessity of being near the Air Ministry and Admiralty, some 140 mi. away from nearest operating airdrome."[144] In Harmon's opinion, this was "objectionable from an inspection and personal contact viewpoint."[145] Because of this arrangement, Harmon more than once emphasized the use of liaison officers to maintain close contact with superior and subordinate units.

---

[142] Harmon Diary in England, 29 & 32.
[143] Harmon Diary in England, 17.
[144] Harmon Diary in England, 19.
[145] Harmon Diary in England, 19.

Specifically, Harmon advocated Naval Liaison officers to help coordinate the anti-shipping efforts and air defense liaison officers to minimize fratricide and work jointly to defend London. Again, this observation would haunt him as the eventual commander of Army Air Forces Pacific Oceans Area. Serving as AAFPOA, the War Department required Harmon to maintain unity of command and synchronization of efforts though his units remained dispersed throughout the 1,000,000 square miles Pacific Oceans Area. In England, long car rides or short plane flights could overcome a 140-mile trek between headquarters and airfields. In the Pacific, the vast distances between bases, coupled with the treacherous navigational challenges posed by open ocean flying, and the constant enemy activity, would make the RAF basing situation appear ideal.

The majority of Harmon's diary entries are favorable regarding RAF war efforts, with the exception of their use of strategic bombers. In fact, Harmon essentially condemned the British appetite for strategic bombing and the policy of non-precision night bombing raids of Germany. During his stay in England, Harmon interviewed numerous RAF officers who lobbied for more American strategic bombers while downplaying a more balanced aviation effort. At many of Harmon's meetings with senior RAF personnel, he noted the majority of discussions were built upon the "need for heavy bombers angle."[146] Harmon wrote on April 16, 1941, that the British were not establishing a prioritized request listing for the procurement of American warplanes. Instead, he wrote, moderately mocking the RAF, were meetings where

---

[146] Harmon Diary in England, 4, 18 & 41.

"everyone says, 'oh, yes, we want heavy bombers,' but no definite priorities are established."[147]

Harmon's first education on the British bombing effort occurred on February 21, 1941, during a visit to 3 Bomber Group and after an in-depth discussion with its commander, Air Vice Marshal Sir John Baldwin, predecessor to Arthur 'Bomber' Harris. During his discussions, it was apparent to Harmon that the British held a "conviction that day bombing won't 'pay its way,'" forcing the British to seek darkness to safeguard the bombers.[148] Later that same day, after a lengthy discussion with an unnamed air commodore, Harmon relayed a conversation that he found very troubling. "The latter [air commodore] made an odd statement," Harmon noted in his diary.[149] "As I recollect to this effect: 'The morale effect of bombing is 9 times the value of the material damage.' And this man is in a responsible staff assignment concerned with the selection of bombardment objectives. I am not too sanguine as to the results of the British effort."[150] In other words, it appeared revenge was a satisfactory goal in and of itself.

Harmon also documented a discussion with the commander of the Air Fighting Development Unit at Duxford. Group Captain G. H. Vasse, eventually promoted to Air Commodore, explained to Miff that with improved training and better tactics, the RAF bombers could restart day bombing efforts with "results more or less commensurate with losses."[151] Harmon replied that American B-17 Flying Fortresses would eventually utilize the particular tactics identified by Vasse. But at 30,000 feet and, of course, with "no

---

[147] Harmon Diary in England, 4, 16 & 41.
[148] Harmon Diary in England, 21.
[149] Harmon Diary in England, 25 – 26.
[150] Harmon Diary in England, 25 – 26.
[151] Harmon Diary in England, 37.

comprehensive data on [high altitude bombing]," the Americans were confident that they "could hit a hell of a lot more and more accurately than either they or the Jerrys [were] hitting at night."[152]

Harmon concluded his fact-finding mission to England in late May 1941, touring some of the industrial areas in Bristol subjected to recent 'Blitz' attacks. Amazed by the apparent destruction wrought by the German bombing efforts, Harmon was perceptive enough to capture the true effectiveness of the enemy air attacks. While noting in his journal many of the bombed buildings and roads in the area, he saw workers were able to seek shelter during air raids in less than five minutes. After sounding the all-clear, factory production could usually resume within twenty minutes. It was obvious to Harmon that industrial bombing efforts against England were ineffective.

Figure 9: London during 'The Blitz.' Life continues in London after a night of German bombing raids. Source: http://encycl.opentopia.com/enimages/thumb/18/17867/0px-LondonBombedWWII.gif, accessed 25 February 2007.

[152] Harmon Diary in England, 37.

On his voyage home from England, Harmon made several unrelated diary entries, which appear to be excerpts of stories, or reflections on conversations had during the six-month assignment. A story of Takoradi, Ghana, reminded Harmon of his days in the Philippines and Mexico and served as a warning for the future. Takoradi stood as one of the main airports servicing the Mediterranean theater, with service predominantly to Cairo. Harmon noted the airfields in Takoradi were small, unimproved, and unusual. Punctuated by extreme temperatures, sandstorms, and high winds, the African area was treacherous for flight operations. "Takoradi and the whole Gold Coast area," Harmon wrote, were "extremely unhealthy with a high incidence of violent malaria."[153] Furthermore, westerners "assigned [in] this area cannot... hold out for longer than about 5 [months]."[154]

Harmon's journeys had taken him full circle by the summer of 1941. Again, the world was at war, and he was but one of a few senior military officers who had seen this conflict firsthand. After living through months of 'The Blitz,' Harmon took his personal experiences home to Washington, DC, eager to inspire the War Department to study the British efforts. He also witnessed the closed-minded nature of some RAF personnel bent on strategic bombing linked to unclear objectives or a confused strategy. In England, Harmon observed the changes in pursuit tactics designed to compensate for the recent rapid technological advancements in small aircraft. High-altitude dogfights and integration with surface defenses had some effectiveness in the daytime and limited effectiveness at night. Harmon noted the need for improved airdromes that were safe from enemy attack. The ability to

---

[153] Harmon Diary in England, Book 3.
[154] Harmon Diary in England, Book 3.

maintain combat aircraft, operate those aircraft predictably while providing for the health and well-being of the men were critical in sustained operations. Finally, as if foreshadowing assignments to come, Harmon again recognized the debilitating nature of expeditionary warfare at places such as Takoradi, where terrain, weather, disease, and poor logistics resulted in high attrition rates for both men and material. These were significant challenges for the British in 1941, but they would be greater obstacles for Harmon in 1942.

Chapter Six: The Road to War

> "...for we are all called upon to create and perfect as rapidly as possible [a] highly efficient Combat Air Force."
>
> *Major General Millard F. Harmon, Jr., Fall 1941*

Returning home after six months of duty might mean a short period of rest for most people, however, Miff Harmon was in great demand. As one of the few senior officers of the Air Corps during a rapid period of growth, Harmon spent the next eight months at four different assignments. Harmon returned to Hamilton Field for a brief respite before the Air Force ordered him south to Riverside, California, as the Commanding General of Interceptor Command and Fourth Air Force. Harmon returned to his pursuit background and assumed responsibility for the defense of the western United States. Promoted to Major General on July 11, 1941, Harmon moved a week later to Fort George Wright in Spokane, Washington, as the Commander of Second Air Force.

He was in command of the Second Air Force for approximately seven months before the Japanese attacked Pearl Harbor. As frenzy swept over the War Department, Harmon again moved and was elevated to the role of Acting Commanding General of Air Force Combat Command (AFCC). Six months earlier, with the revision of Army Regulation 95-5, the War Department had created the Army Air Forces and named General Arnold as its chief. Below Arnold were two organizations, Chief of the Air Corps and Air Force

Combat Command. This new job identified Harmon as one of the most senior Army Air Forces generals at the outset of the war. Air Force Combat Command, formerly known as General Headquarters Air Force, was responsible for the development of air doctrine and operational plans. During his brief period at AFCC, Harmon worked on the design of air theaters, positioning of air assets, and the protection of US-based facilities and airplanes.[155] From the beginning, Harmon knew this job was temporary, and in fact, after a month, Hap Arnold tapped Harmon to be his Chief of the Air Staff, Army Air Forces in Washington, DC.[156] In this position, his last assignment in the United States, Harmon reported directly to Hap Arnold during the opening moves of World War II. In choosing Harmon, Arnold had followed an old practice of familiarity in picking a chief of staff. Miff and Hap had known each other for over thirty years.[157]

In his role as the Chief of the Air Staff, Harmon worked feverishly to manage a growing staff function in the midst of the largest military build-up in American history. The flow of information in and out of Arnold's office required Harmon frequently work well into the night with a second secretarial shift. During this turbulent time, Harmon coordinated the movement of forces throughout the United States, signed orders for the creation of new organizations, and coordinated the deployment of American airmen overseas. In one particularly fascinating instance, Harmon made a fateful decision bearing on America's first blow

---

[155] Transcript, telephone conversation between Major General M.F. Harmon (AFCC) and Colonel Robert G. Breene, 20 Dec 1941, in Millard F. Harmon Personal Papers, 168.604-15, AFHRA.

[156] Harmon and Breene telephone conversation.

[157] H. H. Arnold, *Global Mission* (New York: Harper & Brothers Publishers, 1949), 338.

against the Empire of Japan. For months, Lieutenant Colonel James 'Jimmy' Doolittle had worked with a small group of aviators and support personnel to develop plans that would enable a strike against mainland Japan. As the planning and practicing reached its culmination, Doolittle visited Arnold's office in Washington, DC, for final coordination. At this moment, the Army had still not chosen anyone to lead the fateful raid, and Doolittle pressed Arnold for permission. Arnold, in an attempt to stall Doolittle or table the discussion temporarily, told Doolittle to ask Miff for permission. In a mad sprint through the halls of the War Department, Doolittle arrived in Harmon's office and asked to lead the mission. Doolittle said, "Miff, I've just been to see Hap about the project I've been working on and said I wanted to lead the mission. Hap said it was okay with him if it's okay with you."[158] Harmon approved. Only seconds later, as Doolittle sprinted out of Harmon's office, Arnold's voice piped in over the call box, asking Miff not to make a decision regarding Doolittle. Miff replied, "But Hap, I told him he could go."[159]

Who's in Charge?

Prior to Doolittle's raid in April 1942, a turf war had begun in the Pacific between the Army and the Navy over the delineation of responsibilities and command relationships for the war against Japan. At odds were two personality juggernauts, Army General Douglas MacArthur and Navy Admiral Chester Nimitz. In a compromise, the War Department charged General MacArthur with the defense of the Southwest Pacific Area (SWPA), including

---

[158] James H. Doolittle and Carroll V. Glines, *I Could Never Be So Lucky Again: An Autobiography by General James H. "Jimmy" Doolittle* (New York: Bantam Books, 1991), 249.
[159] Doolittle and Glines, *I Could Never Be So Lucky Again,* 249.

Australia, New Zealand, and the Philippines. Admiral Nimitz, Commander in Chief Pacific Oceans Areas (CINCPOA), assumed responsibility for the bulk of the remaining Pacific region, a massive undertaking requiring a further division into three smaller areas: North, Central, and South Pacific Ocean Areas (SOPAC). Nimitz appointed Vice Admiral (VADM) Robert L. Ghormley as Commander SOPAC (COMSOPAC) while retaining direct control of the central Pacific himself.[160]

This organizational structure did not solve many of the growing command problems in the Pacific. Because there was no single authority throughout the entire Pacific theater, MacArthur and Nimitz negotiated much of the strategic planning and the resolution of greater operational conflicts. On many occasions, the Joint Chiefs of Staff in Washington, DC, had to referee competing requests that eventually spiraled into a constant struggle for limited resources, particularly as they related to troop carriers, aircraft, and ships.[161]

At the beginning of direct US involvement in World War II, the Army had approximately 60,000 troops and a few aircraft squadrons scattered throughout the vast Pacific.[162] In a theater where many installations were nearly 3,000 miles apart and with shipping between those locations at an absolute

---

[160] For further discussion of this quarrel, read Louis Morton, *United States Army in World War II, The War in the Pacific, Strategy and Command: The First Two Years* (1962; new imprint, Washington, DC: Center of Military History, 2000).
[161] Louis Morton, *United States Army in World War II, The War in the Pacific, Strategy and Command: The First Two Years* (1962; new imprint, Washington, DC: Center of Military History, 2000), 250.
[162] Morton, *Strategy and Command*, 256.

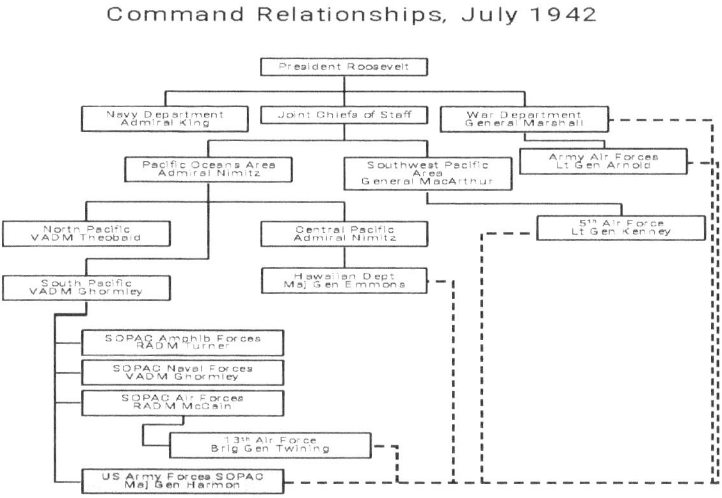

Figure 10: Command Relationships in 1942. Source: Louis Morton, United States Army in World War II, The War in the Pacific, Strategy, and Command: The First Two Years (1962; new imprint, Washington, DC: Center of Military History, 2000), 254. Modified by the author.

premium, an Army commander with superior organizational skills was required. Additionally, this commander would need to possess the most acute joint warfighting skills available. In September 1942, one hundred and three officers comprised Admiral Ghormley's headquarters, responsible for all joint operations and planning. Of those officers, only three were Army officers.[163] To make matters more challenging, both Nimitz and MacArthur demanded more Army Air Forces planes, in particular their newest bombers, the B-17 Flying Fortress. Yet throughout the Pacific, Army and Air Force planners, backed by President Roosevelt, prevented

[163] Morton, *Strategy and Command*, 257.

the establishment of a heavy bombardment arm in the South Pacific.[164]

General Marshall recognized the growing need for Army leadership in a predominantly naval theater. In addition, Marshall knew this Army officer would require first-hand knowledge regarding the employment of Army Air Forces in support of naval operations. Following intense discussions between General Dwight Eisenhower, Admiral Ernest King, Admiral Ghormley, Harmon, and Marshall, Marshall appointed Harmon the Commanding General, United States Army Forces in the South Pacific Area (USAFISPA) with the shorter title of Commanding General South Pacific (COMGENSOPAC).[165] On July 7, 1942, Marshall told Harmon that his responsibilities were the administration, organization, supply, and training of all Army bases, ground, and air units in the South Pacific area.[166]

Additionally, Harmon was to assist Ghormley in the preparation and execution of any developing operations. Prior to these activities, Marshall told Harmon to survey the South Pacific area and submit a detailed report regarding the state of affairs and make recommendations as appropriate. Before departing to Washington, DC, Harmon visited many of the major "Army and naval agencies in order to familiarize himself" with his pending

---

[164] Morton, *Strategy and Command*, 258.
[165] Morton, *Strategy and Command*, 260.
[166] Report, "The Army in the South Pacific" with references by Millard F. Harmon, Jr., 6 Jun 1944, Marshall to Harmon, Letter of Instructions to the Commanding General, U.S. Army Forces in the South Pacific Area, 7 July 1942, in Millard F. Harmon, Jr. Papers, 705.04A, IRIS No. 0251243, AFHRA. (Hereafter cited as "Harmon, *Army in the South Pacific*").

assignment.[167] He spent the last few days with his family before leaving for California, and on July 21, 1942, along with General George Kenney, Harmon departed Hamilton Field for Hawaii.[168]

Figure 11: SOPAC Campaign Planning. September 1942, discussing operations in the Solomons with Admiral Nimitz (seated). Standing is General Patch (left), Admiral Ghormley (center), and Major General Harmon (right). Source: Louis Morton, United States Army in World War II, The War In the Pacific, Strategy, and Command: The First Two Years (1962; new imprint, Washington, DC: Center of Military History, 2000), 339.

---

[167] Wesley Frank Craven and James Lea Cate, eds., *The Army Air Forces in World War II, vol. 4, The Pacific – Guadalcanal to Saipan, August 1942 to July 1944* (Chicago, IL: University of Chicago Press, 1950), 32.

[168] George Kenney, *General Kenney Reports* (New York: Duell, Sloan and Pearce, 1949), 19.

State of Affairs in the Pacific

> "In a nutshell, if full effectiveness of combat forces is to be realized there must be available service troops to take care of the many activities, non-combat in character. Each one of these island forces, and bear in mind that many of the islands are quite large, is a miniature theater of operations."
>
> *Major General Millard F. Harmon, Jr., August 11, 1942*

Miff Harmon was no stranger to the Pacific. In fact, he had already spent many of his formative years in this vast area of operations. His first overseas assignment in the Philippines and his major command tour at Luke Field prepared Harmon for many of the Pacific's idiosyncrasies. Prior to departing for the South Pacific, Harmon selected key members of his future staff. Harmon chose Brigadier General Nathan F. Twining as his Chief of Staff, Colonels Robert G. Breene as his Chief of Supply, Dean C. Strother, Thomas D. Roberts, and Frank F. Everest as his aircraft operations officers, and Francis T. Ankenbrandt as his signal officer. Seven of the original nine men selected by Harmon were Air Force officers, and most served with him during earlier assignments.[169] These men left in advance while Harmon stopped in the Fijis on July 26 before arriving in Noumea, New Caledonia, and opening his headquarters on July 29.[170] Harmon's decision to base his headquarters in Noumea was in contradiction to his first orders to establish operations in Auckland, New Zealand. Harmon felt New Zealand was too far from the developing operations, so he established his

---

[169] Craven and Cate, *The Pacific – Guadalcanal to Saipan*, 32.
[170] Morton, *Strategy and Command*, 261.

forward headquarters in Noumea, leaving Breene behind in New Zealand as his rear echelon representative.[171]

Harmon's trip from the US foreshadowed the tough job ahead of him. Having flown for hours and radioed ahead several times, Harmon expected a small welcoming party to meet his aircraft upon landing in the Fiji Islands. However, as Harmon and Kenney deplaned, it took fifteen minutes before a young lieutenant arrived to greet them. The lieutenant presented Harmon with a note from the base commander stating he was unable to greet the general because he was preoccupied with a sunbath.[172] Harmon and Kenney left for the chow hall, and one week later, Harmon relieved the base commander.[173]

Harmon's theater and his minor forces were essentially thrown together overnight. In the organizational spasm following the attack on Pearl Harbor, the Army dispersed thousands of soldiers throughout the one million-square mile Pacific theater to garrison remaining US interests that had yet fallen to Japanese offensives. The Army left these forces with poor supplies, convoluted command arraignments, and confusing mission orders. Troops in the South Pacific were scattered through New Zealand, New Caledonia, Efate, and Espiritu Santo in the New Hebrides, the Fijis, Tongatabu, and Bora Bora.[174] Harmon had the Americal Division on New Caledonia, the majority of the 37th Division in Fiji, the 147th Infantry in Tongatabu, and most of the 102nd Infantry Regiment in Bora Bora.[175]

---

[171] Harmon, *Army in the South Pacific*, 1.
[172] Kenney, *General Kenney Reports*, 20.
[173] Kenney, *General Kenney Reports*, 20 – 21.
[174] Morton, *Strategy and Command*, 257.
[175] Harmon, *Army in the South Pacific*, 1.

Harmon's air forces, which reported to Admiral John McCain for operational control, were also in a sad state of readiness and lacked any new aircraft other than a handful of B-17s from the 11th Bombardment Group.[176] The Army's air forces included two fighter squadrons and two medium bombardment squadrons divided between Fiji and New Caledonia.[177] Many of the airfields used by the Army Air Forces were horribly unprepared and subjected to some of the harshest weather conditions on the planet. Harmon characterized his "facilities during this period [as] meager in the extreme."[178] Airfields remained hundreds of miles apart with limited supply capabilities or local infrastructures to leverage. In one instance, the newly formed 67th Fighter Squadron, organized to fight with the Bell P-39 Airacobra, arrived in Noumea to find the Army had mistakenly shipped P-400s instead of P-39s. The "Fighting Cocks" maintenance personnel and pilots assembled their 'new' aircraft and began to fly combat missions within a few short weeks.[179]✪ Only through sheer will would many soldiers assigned to this new theater survive the initial months.

---

[176] Harmon, *Army in the South Pacific*, 2.
[177] Harmon, *Army in the South Pacific*, 2.
[178] Harmon, *Army in the South Pacific*, 2.
[179] The 67th Fighter Squadron, "Fighting Cocks," stood up at Selfridge Field, MI shortly after the attack on Pearl Harbor. After only a few weeks, the Army deployed the 'Cocks' to Australia and told them to leave their aircraft behind in the states. The Army promised new aircraft once they arrived at their deployed location. The 'Cocks' spent only a few weeks in Australia before they loaded aboard ships and departed for New Caledonia. Arriving on the island on 15 Mar 1942, they found several wooden crates waiting for them. The lack of modern transportation infrastructure meant many personnel carried some of the crates to a mud strip on the opposite side of the island. Once they opened their crates, the 'Cocks' found P-400s instead of their familiar P-39 Airacobras. The P-400 was the export variant of the Airacobra, and while similar in appearances, the aircraft performed differently. Maintenance personnel went to work on the unfamiliar aircraft and pilots studied what manuals they could find. Shortly

Upon arrival in his new theater, Harmon set to work evaluating the state of affairs and preparing his report to Marshall as ordered. As a "thumb nail sketch" submitted to explain briefly the situation and serve as a precursor to further requests, Harmon began his report with a simple sentence. "I did not realize and I doubt if many in Washington do, the size of these islands and the difficulties of communication." Harmon surveyed operations in the Fijis, New Caledonia, Efate, Espiritu Santo, the Santa Cruz group, and finally, Guadalcanal. At each location, he outlined the forces, port facilities, possible airfield locations, available workforce, and radar sites.

Although Marshall had told Harmon to report on the entire Army operations, it was evident from the report that Miff focused predominantly on the air situation throughout his theater. It is unknown but doubtful if he filed a separate report specifically detailing the ground estimate of the situation. On the other hand, it may be the air situation in the South Pacific required more attention than his ground forces. In either case, Harmon's report on the status of his aviation capabilities is detailed and thorough. Harmon identified airfield requirements at each location, and the preponderance of those requests focused on construction and runway improvements. Harmon visited seven different airfields and noted airfield surfaces were all sod except one oiled dirt runway.[180] These conditions, considering an average annual rainfall

---

thereafter, the 'Cocks' deployed again to Guadalcanal. The flight to Guadalcanal involved intermediate stops at Efate and Espiritu Santo. It also required adding wing tanks and the escort of a B-17 bomber because the P-400 lacked sufficient navigation equipment. The 'Cocks' arrived at Henderson Field, Guadalcanal and became the first Army Air Forces unit of the "Cactus Air Force." Commanding this legendary unit was a professional highlight for me.

[180] "Narrative - Notes on Bases of the Army, South Pacific (exclusive of Bora Bora, Tongatabu, etc), 11 Aug 1942" by Major General Millard F. Harmon, Jr., General Historical & Operational Reports, 98-USF2-0.6, Record Group 338,

in some islands exceeded 160 inches, were unsatisfactory and required immediate attention.[181] Unlike the paved British airfields Harmon visited in 1941, Miff's theater consisted of unimproved jungle airstrips, non-existent logistical infrastructure, and intense tropical weather.

To overcome these challenges, Miff requested a significant increase in labor. Harmon wrote the "difficulties of transportation" in this widely dispersed theater put a significant premium on competent workers.[182] Harmon tried to employ many of the local islanders to complement his slim forces but found most of the available laborers incapable in the tasks required. Complicating matters were the numerous languages and cultural barriers that varied from island to island. Similar to his initial experiences in the Philippines, where terrain and water segregated many areas into non-homogeneous pockets of Filipinos, the South Pacific was even more difficult due to the vast expanses and limited transportation resources.

Harmon also saw potential problems with the prevalence of insect-borne diseases.[183] Having witnessed firsthand the problems of malaria in the Philippines or the devastation wrought on the coast of Africa, Harmon knew that American soldiers would have higher attrition rates due to sickness than the local population. Coupled with the difficult terrain, harsh weather, and potential enemy action, Harmon's theater required a much greater logistical emphasis than anything he had seen before. Admiral McCain,

---

National Archives, College Park, MD, 4. (Hereafter cited as "Harmon, Notes on Bases").

[181] Harmon, Notes on Bases, 4.
[182] Harmon, Notes on Bases, 5.
[183] Harmon, Notes on Bases, 6.

commander of all air forces in the South Pacific (COMAIRSOPAC), also recognized these problems. McCain decided that "it was entirely impracticable for him to exercise his command directly," and set out to delineate mission responsibilities with Harmon.[184] McCain determined the doctrine and use of all air forces but delegated the training and preparation for those missions to Harmon. Harmon then used his individual island commanders to execute operations in accordance with McCain's plan.

Admiral McCain was not impressive as a combat air planner. According to Hap Arnold's New Caledonia diary from September 1942, Arnold wrote McCain's discussion of airpower revolved solely around Army Air Forces aircraft. "Take the United States Army Air experiences out of McCain's talk, and there is nothing left."[185] Arnold felt that McCain was unable to devise a competent air plan for the South Pacific and relegated strategic aircraft, such as the B-17, to patrol duties better left for Navy PBYs. Harmon also felt that the current command arrangements in the South Pacific led to inefficiencies in the application of joint airpower. After meeting with Admiral Nimitz on his way to Noumea, Harmon expressed these concerns specifically. Miff "held strong reservations as to the wisdom of sacrificing operational control over the air units."[186] However, his loyalty to his commanders and his professionalism as an officer prevented him from pursuing the matter further. Miff held his criticisms and supported the mission as ordered.[187] Nimitz respected Harmon's position and wrote a supportive

---

[184] Craven and Cate, *The Pacific – Guadalcanal to Saipan*, 30.
[185] John W. Huston *America's Airpower Comes of Age: General Henry H. "Hap" Arnold's World War II Diaries* (Maxwell AFB, AL: Air University Press, 2002), 389.
[186] Craven and Cate, *The Pacific – Guadalcanal to Saipan*, 33.
[187] Craven and Cate, *The Pacific – Guadalcanal to Saipan*, 33.

recommendation to McCain in advance of Harmon's arrival in the theater in an attempt to alleviate any fears.[188]

By the first week in August 1942, Harmon had completed his assessment and established his headquarters in Noumea. He understood his limited role in the predominantly naval theater and recognized that the lack of air experience in the current command structure warranted his valuable inputs. Harmon also realized all of his individual units and, more importantly, the whole South Pacific required immediate resupply. The limited fighter aircraft available to Harmon were unable to meet what he expected to be the same type of aerial combat that he had seen in Britain between the RAF and the Luftwaffe. The underpowered and lightly armored P-39s and P-400s would be no match for the Japanese Zeros if the two were to meet in the near future. Additionally, Harmon's theater required an urgent injection of transport aircraft, both large and small machines, to deliver supplies between the isolated island outposts.

Harmon's orders from Marshall, restricting him to only administrative control over his forces, were also very broad and subject to individual interpretation.[189] Whereas most soldiers might be inclined to remain within established bounds, Miff recognized the many grey areas and the pressing requirements for

---

[188] Admiral Chester W. Nimitz, Commander in Chief, Pacific, to Rear Admiral John S. McCain, Commander, Air, South Pacific, letter, 27 July 1942, Admiral Nimitz Collection, Admiral's Letters – 1942, Series XIII, Early Records Collection, Operational Archives Branch, Naval Historical Center, Washington, DC. Nimitz told McCain, "Harmon fully appreciates the fact that you are to continue to exercise operational control of all air components in the South Pacific. In my opinion, Harmon is a first-rate selection for the job, and I feel sure that you will work harmoniously together. (No pun intended!)" Underlined emphasis in the original.

[189] Morton, *Strategy and Command*, 261.

Figure 12: P-38 Lightnings arrive. Harmon's unassembled P-38s being delivered to New Caledonia through the streets of Noumea, September 1942. Source: Louis Morton, United States Army in World War II, The War in the Pacific, Strategy and Command: The First Two Years (1962; new imprint, Washington, DC: Center of Military History, 2000), 332.

his forces. As such, Harmon stretched his scope of authority and aggressively sought answers to many of his problems. Playing a more operational role than his orders envisioned, Harmon set out to requisition as many new aircraft and personnel for his theater as possible.[190] Harmon's understanding of the Army Air Forces system, and his recent position as Chief of the Air Staff in Washington, DC, gave him unique insight into the tumultuous supply demands being placed on the Army and potential inroads to turn that tumult to the South Pacific's advantage.

Initially, the War Department delayed or denied many of Harmon's requests for reinforcements. By late July 1942, a large build-up of weapons in England, combined with a policy of keeping

---

[190] Morton, *Strategy and Command*, 261.

the Pacific Theater held to the 'minimum' necessary to maintain a defensive posture, meant limited assets available for Harmon and Ghormley.[191] On August 5, however, after receiving several denials, Admiral King pushed Harmon's newest request to Marshall. Harmon, through Admiral Ghormley, requested the Army rush a massive influx of men and material to the South Pacific, a request he knew would be hard to fill. Harmon estimated he needed six more fighter squadrons, three of which should be equipped with the new Lockheed P-38 Lightning.[192] Additionally, Miff needed two more heavy, one medium, and three dive-bomber squadrons. A total of four antiaircraft regiments and harbor defense artillery units, plus two 105-mm howitzer coastal artillery outfits, were necessary for the defense of the many airfields and undefended ports.[193]

On August 7th, a mere nine days after Harmon arrived in theater, the Marines invaded Guadalcanal and Tulagi in the Solomon Islands. Under the support of Army bombers, Marine and Navy fighters, plus naval gunfire support, the United States landed its first soldiers on enemy-occupied territory and began to strike back at Japan. For a moment, enemy resistance was nonexistent, and most of the Marines made their landings without opposition. Major General Alexander Vandegrift, commander of the 1st Marine Division ashore on Guadalcanal, adjusted his scheme of maneuver to attack toward Lunga instead of the originally targeted Mount Austin.[194] The Marines' first hours on the hot and oppressively

---

[191] Morton, *Strategy and Command*, 322.
[192] Morton, *Strategy and Command*, 322.
[193] Morton, *Strategy and Command*, 322.
[194] John Miller, Jr. *United States Army in World War II, The War in the Pacific, Guadalcanal: The First Offensive* (Washington, DC: Department of the Army, 1949), 71.

humid island had begun to take their toll, slowing the advance more than expected. Lunga also was the location of the main Japanese airfield on the island, fit for reinforcement by Japanese aircraft unless the Marines arrived first. According to Miff Harmon, Lunga airfield, later known as Henderson Field, would be the center of gravity for the entire operation.

Chapter Seven: Miff Harmon Strikes Back

"Miff was one of the few people who was tactically sound and had done a lot of thinking on this matter. Knew how to use airpower and had good solid views on it and encouraged everyone else to develop this knowledge and the know how."

General Dean C. Strother, April 1976

"Situation Cactus[195] extremely grave. Air operations from that base seriously curtailed. Airdrome area continues subject to land-based and ship borne artillery fire. Jap forces ashore estimated about fifteen thousand. Ours approximately twenty three thousand, and not fully effective."

War Department Message, Harmon to Marshall,

October 17, 1942

During the two months preceding the Marine landing on Guadalcanal, Army Air Forces and Naval aircraft conducted maritime patrols, reconnaissance missions, and limited attack against the island in preparation for an August invasion. On several reconnaissance patrols over Guadalcanal, the Americans noted

---

[195] Cactus was the codename for Guadalcanal.

extensive Japanese efforts to clear a large area on the north side of the island and reinforce that area with men and construction equipment. Completion of the Lunga Point airstrip meant Japanese long-range aircraft could threaten the main lines of communication between the United States and Australia. North of Guadalcanal, Japanese forces were finishing other airfields and fortifying major installations to support combat operations further into the Solomons. In particular, the Japanese base at Rabaul, New Britain, stood as a major foothold in the South Pacific.

Success at Guadalcanal, and eventually the remainder of the Solomons, relied heavily on the ability to operate as many aircraft as possible — ship-based or shore-based — in support operations ashore. Late in the planning process, Admiral Ghormley recognized this fact and emphasized the need to develop airfields along the route of advance that could enable forces to "leap distances of 150 to 200 miles."[196] Unfortunately, because the Army Air Forces had yet to materialize and the infrastructure to support operations was immature, Ghormley felt his ship-based aviation could provide the initial support. Until Harmon's arrival in theater, Army participation in the form of land-based aircraft was suspect at best. In fact, Ghormley was unsure if land-based aviation would be available for the invasion.[197] Admiral McCain also recognized this potential obstacle. "The Army apparently is taking no interest in this area," McCain wrote to Ghormley. "Seemingly we are not going to get any planes and seemingly also a string will be tied to those we have. I suggest you work it up with the New Zealand government to make

---

[196] Vice Admiral Robert L. Ghormley, Commander, South Pacific, to Admiral Chester W. Nimitz, Commander in Chief, Pacific, letter, 29 July 1942, Admiral Nimitz Collection, Admiral's Letters – 1942, Series XIII, Early Records Collection, Operational Archives Branch, Naval Historical Center, Washington, DC.
[197] Ghormley to Nimitz, July 29, 1942.

a strong bid for the acquisition, through Lend-Lease of 20 B-17s, 36 B-26s, 26 dive bombers, latest model, and 36 fighters, latest model."[198] This plea underscored friction between Army and Navy planners regarding the South Pacific. McCain was desperate enough to seek assistance from other Allied governments.

What little land-based aviation that did arrive lacked a potent punch. Harmon's principal long-range strike aircraft, the Boeing B-17 Flying Fortress, was the only plane able to accomplish surface search missions and area reconnaissance because of its great range and defensive armament. Consequently, the Navy assigned the B-17s this non-traditional task. Harmon's medium-range bombers, Martin B-26 Marauders, stationed in the New Hebrides and Fijians, were unable to reach Guadalcanal and therefore relegated to local island defense. Army Air Forces fighter aircraft, totaling a meager fourteen P-400 single-engine light fighters by the end of August, could not operate from Guadalcanal until the airfield was secure and parts, fuel, equipment, and ammunition were in place.

Despite the unsettled air situation, Admiral Ghormley, in accordance with directives from the Joint Chiefs of Staff, ordered the invasion of Guadalcanal to proceed on August 7, 1942. Initially, the Marines met little resistance as they established a beachhead and captured the Japanese airfield, promptly renaming it Henderson Field. For weeks thereafter, the dearth of heavy aircraft and dangerous conditions at Henderson made airlift supply missions unrealistic. Accordingly, support at Guadalcanal relied on Naval forces, whose efforts were likewise constrained by poor port

---

[198] Rear Admiral John S. McCain, Commander, Air, South Pacific, to Vice Admiral Robert L. Ghormley, Commander, South Pacific, letter, 6 July 1942, Vice Admiral Robert L. Ghormley Papers, Early Records Collection, Operational Archives Branch, Naval Historical Center, Washington, DC.

facilities and the use of slow, non-maneuverable, flat-bottom ships. During these operations, supply ships required surface fleet protection and air cover to ward off enemy efforts to interdict supplies. Unfortunately, after less than twenty-four hours into the operation, the Japanese navy scored a grand victory.

Under the cover of darkness on August 8th, a sizeable Japanese naval task force was able to enter, undetected by US forces, the narrow, protected water passage known as the "Slot." Upon sailing into the area, Japanese naval combatants routed US naval forces, ultimately forcing the US Navy task force commander, Vice Admiral Frank Fletcher, to order withdrawal. In the end, several Allied warships were lost, and for the moment, the Marines ashore on Guadalcanal lacked critical supplies. Basing American shore-based aircraft on Guadalcanal would have to wait another two weeks before the field was completed. The Marines and a handful of Navy Seabees, stranded with no construction equipment and limited supplies, began construction on the airfield using shovels and, on some occasions, bare hands.

The progress of operations ashore was disappointing, and the naval disaster at Savo Island was a significant setback. Writing to Admiral Nimitz three days later, Ghormley conceded the "loss of those ships the other evening [was] hard to take."[199] Furthermore, he believed that "surface ships cannot operate, especially in very restricted waters, where they are subject to attack by shore-based aircraft."[200] Accelerating efforts at Henderson Field was the only

---

[199] Vice Admiral Robert L. Ghormley, Commander, South Pacific, to Admiral Chester W. Nimitz, Commander in Chief, Pacific, letter, 11 August 1942, Admiral Nimitz Collection, Admiral's Letters – 1942, Series XIII, Early Records Collection, Operational Archives Branch, Naval Historical Center, Washington, DC.

[200] Ghormley to Nimitz, 11 August 1942.

remedy available. To deter Japanese shore-based aircraft, defensive fighters needed a completed airstrip. Only then could fighter aircraft protect the Navy's ships.

According to Harmon, the slow progress of work on Henderson stemmed from naval failures at logistical planning. In a letter to Hap Arnold in early September, Harmon identified poor prioritization of airfield construction equipment on the invasion barges. The Navy had misconstrued the true nature of the operation, Harmon believed. Success in the Solomons could only happen if land-based air operations were effective, and Harmon argued that seizure and improvement of the Lunga airstrip should have been the first priority. However, the Navy viewed the landings as an amphibious effort and "not as a means of establishing strong land-based air operations."[201] The lack of prioritization, combined with the stunning naval defeat and subsequent retreat of US Naval forces, meant additional supplies such as fuel, runway matting, and even food for the workers were in critically short supply.

"This Logistic Support Thing"[202]

Harmon had learned at a very young age that building and supporting aviation operations, especially in harsh conditions, rested upon a foundation of sound logistics. The Navy's logistical concerns depended heavily on modern ports, refueling ships, and supply vessels. The notion of building an active land-based airfield was foreign to Navy planners, and the late addition of Harmon to

---

[201] John Miller, Jr. *United States Army in World War II, The War in the Pacific, Guadalcanal: The First Offensive* (Washington, DC: Department of the Army, 1949), 85.

[202] General Nathan F. Twining, interview by Dr. Murray Green, 3 November 1967, transcript, Box 9, Addendum 19, The Murray Green Collection, US Air Force Academy Library, Colorado Springs, CO.

the operational planning was unable to overcome the existing shortsightedness.

Much of the blame for these logistical limits falls squarely on Admiral Ghormley's shoulders. Ghormley recognized that the South Pacific Theater would pose significant logistical constraints on his naval forces, but he failed to consider the other aspects of his command. Ghormley's letter to Nimitz on August 11 simply states the obvious: "This island warfare is a tough nut. The shipping problem is difficult. We need big transport planes."[203] Ghormley correctly identified critical problems but failed to offer solutions. Instead, he relied on Nimitz. In a post-war interview, when asked if Ghormley understood logistical concerns in his theater, General Nathan Twining responded with a startling story. "One day, we are out there talking and Ghormley turns to me and said, 'you know, I've been thinking this over' he said, 'there is something to this logistic support thing, isn't there?'"[204] For Twining, it was an "unbelievable" admission from the SOPAC commander.[205]

Hap Arnold recognized these problems during his visit to the South Pacific in mid-September. Arnold wrote scathing criticisms of the Navy's method of supply operations in his diary and even called into question the fighting spirit of the theater commanders. Arnold wrote the Navy needed a "shot in the arm" at Guadalcanal, and that shot could only come from "leaders who know and understand modern warfare, men who are aggressive, who are not afraid to fight their ships."[206] Furthermore, Arnold noted the "Navy has no

---

[203] Ghormley to Nimitz, 11 August 1942.
[204] Twining, interview, 3 November 1967.
[205] Twining, interview, 3 November 1967.
[206] John W. Huston, *America's Airpower Comes of Age: General Henry H. 'Hap' Arnold's World War II Diaries,* vol. 1 (Maxwell AFB, AL: Air University Press, 2002), 381.

conception of supplies, installations, and facilities required to operate land-based aircraft."[207]

Harmon's initial orders from the War Department charged him with the "supply of all [Army] bases in [the South Pacific]."[208] However, his supply network was ultimately reliant on the San Francisco Port of Embarkation and the priorities established by COMSOPAC. "Delivery of supplies" was made "in full shipload lots to the respective bases in accordance with the directives of COMSOPAC for supplies procured by the Joint Purchasing Board."[209] In sum, Harmon established Army requests and then waited patiently for the Navy to deliver. The Navy did not address this problem until late October and only after SOPAC was under new leadership.

Hap Arnold's War by Algebra

Harmon ultimately had to make do with the limited resources he was given. Henderson Field accepted aircraft on August 20 and welcomed thirty-one Marine and Navy fighters. Two days later, the first five Army P-400s from the 67th Fighter Squadron arrived to join the 'Cactus Air Force' under the command of Brigadier General Roy Geiger's 1st Marine Aviation Wing.[210] Four days later, an additional nine P-400s brought the total to fourteen Army Air Forces fighter planes. Unfortunately, initial operations with the P-400s on Guadalcanal were disastrous. Harmon knew in advance

---

[207] Huston, *America's Airpower Comes of Age*, 385. Arnold further wrote, "Ghormley is worried about logistics of operations. Has 80 ships in harbor here that he can't unload. Patch is very insistent that Navy had no plan of logistics."
[208] Harmon, *Army in the South Pacific*, 2.
[209] Marshall to Harmon, 7 July 1942, 3.
[210] Wesley Frank Craven and James Lea Cate, eds., *The Army Air Forces in World War II, vol. 4, The Pacific – Guadalcanal to Saipan, August 1942 to July 1944* (Chicago, IL: University of Chicago Press, 1950), 86.

that tropical conditions and limited supplies were sure to exact a toll similar to his experiences in Mexico with the 1st Aero Squadron. After only four days of combat operations, the enemy had downed four P-400s, nine were broken, and the remaining fighters was barely serviceable.[211]

The situation at the airfield failed to improve rapidly. Supplies were so short that pilots and mechanics pumped fuel by hand into aircraft between sporadic firefights with the enemy along the airfield perimeter. Artillery routinely shelled the airfield, and living conditions were primitive. Airborne, the P-400 was no match for the enemy Mitsubishi Zero fighters. The P-400's service ceiling barely touched 12,000 feet, and the lightly armored engine cowling and limited armaments put American pilots at quite a disadvantage.

Harmon's recognition of the changing nature of air combat during his observation mission to England in 1941 had come full circle. His substandard aircraft were unable to match the enemy in the sky, and the extreme situation on the ground only complicated matters. Immediately, Harmon petitioned Ghormley and Arnold for new fighters, in particular, the Lockheed P-38 Lightning. Ghormley relayed Harmon's concerns to Nimitz. The "P-38 is ideal for this job," he told Nimitz, "but we have none and none in prospect."[212] Harmon's combat experience told him that the power, speed, altitude performance, and second engine for long, over-water

---

[211] Vice Admiral Robert L. Ghormley, Commander, South Pacific, to Admiral Chester W. Nimitz, Commander in Chief, Pacific, letter, 7 September 1942, Admiral Nimitz Collection, Admiral's Letters – 1942, Series XIII, Early Records Collection, Operational Archives Branch, Naval Historical Center, Washington, DC.

[212] Ghormley to Nimitz, 11 August 1942.

flights made the P-38 the logical choice for the South Pacific.[213] Harmon wrote to Arnold on September 15, stating P-400s are "completely ineffective as high-altitude fighters. They simply cannot function at the altitudes at which Jap bombers operate, and are of limited value as medium altitude fighters, but they have done a splendid job as attack."[214]

Hap Arnold was not pleased with the state of affairs in the South Pacific or the incessant requests for what he felt were more aircraft than necessary. As a result, he decided to measure the situation firsthand and left for the region in mid-September on a fact-finding trip. Prior to departing Washington, DC, Arnold had been reminding others of the need to keep 'Germany first' when determining the allocation of limited resources. The United States Army Air Forces were fighting in Europe, the South Pacific, and the Southwest Pacific while preparing to fight in North Africa and simultaneously improving defenses in Hawaii, Alaska, and the continental United States. Arnold was convinced the South Pacific had the required forces necessary to accomplish the mission. That mission, as Arnold often said, was defensive in nature and should be held at the minimum force necessary. Even as the dark specter of defeat loomed over Guadalcanal, Arnold wrote that the "large offensive air force" operations against Germany represented the "first major effort in the war."[215] He further stated it was of the "utmost importance that everything possible be done to ensure its

---

[213] Ghormley to Nimitz, 7 September 1942.
[214] Notes from Murray Green collection, *"Suitability" of the P-400 and P-39 – September 1942*, L/C Box 88, The Murray Green Collection, US Air Force Academy Library, Colorado Springs, CO.
[215] Lieutenant General H.H. Arnold, Commanding General, Army Air Forces, to General G.C. Marshall, Chief of Staff, War Department, memorandum, "North African Operations," 19 August 1942, Box 186, in The Papers of Henry H. Arnold, Library of Congress, Washington, DC.

success," which undoubtedly meant the pooling of more air forces in Europe, not in the Pacific.[216]

Arnold responded to the requests from the Pacific by outlining to the War Department what he believed to be a numerical advantage of aircraft in a tertiary theater, wasted by those who did not understand airpower. "The Japs have put 300 airplanes" into the South and Southwest Pacific Theaters, compared to "500 airplanes in Australia, over 130 airplanes in the Pacific Islands, and 240 airplanes in Hawaii."[217] Arnold wrote that all of these aircraft could concentrate at a critical point, anywhere within the theater, within thirty-six hours.[218] Arnold's argument completely ignored the South Pacific's supply difficulties, poor airfields, and the qualitative advantage enjoyed by Japanese pilots. Furthermore, Arnold believed "everyone agrees that success in the Pacific Theater will not win the war."[219] Yet, "we are planning to concentrate more airplanes there in spite of the very serious shortage which will exist" in other more important operations.[220] "If decisive results are ever to be attained in this war, offensive operations against the center of Axis strength, industrial Germany, must be continued relentlessly from now on, and from every possible base."[221]

On the same day, Arnold wrote to Major General Carl 'Tooey' Spaatz, Commanding General of Eighth Air Force and responsible for the strategic bombardment of industrial Germany. Arnold told Spaatz that the "tendency of the Strategic Planners to take aircraft

---

[216] Arnold to Marshall, 19 August 1942.
[217] Arnold to Marshall, 19 August 1942.
[218] Arnold to Marshall, 19 August 1942.
[219] Arnold to Marshall, 19 August 1942.
[220] Arnold to Marshall, 19 August 1942.
[221] Arnold to Marshall, 19 August 1942, emphasis in the original document.

away from the European Theater and throw it in the Southwest Pacific" was very disturbing.[222] Arnold exhorted Spaatz and other Allied commanders in London to clamor for more planes. Arnold told Spaatz to get Dwight Eisenhower and Arthur Portal to "stand up on their hind legs for the Air Force that is needed" to defeat Germany.[223] Spaatz agreed with Arnold's assertion, writing to a member of Arnold's staff that "if we only had a couple of hundred B-17's here now instead of scattered all over the world, we could come pretty close to giving the Germans a knockout blow."[224] Twelve days later, Spaatz sent a more pointed message stating the "diversion of Air Forces destined for this theater to another theater prevents essential exploitation of present German position in the air and jeopardizes ultimate victory."[225]

In September 1942, Army Air Forces were engaged in two major theaters, the European Theater, with an emphasis on daylight, precision bombing, and the Pacific Theater, with an emphasis on airpower subordinated to support land and naval forces. The immature industrial nature of the Pacific Theater did not present valuable targets for destruction by Army Air Forces strategic bombers. Moreover, the battle in the Pacific tended to subjugate

---

[222] Lieutenant General H.H. Arnold, Commanding General, Army Air Forces, to Major General C.A. Spaatz, Commanding General, Eighth Air Force, letter, 19 August 1942, Box 186, in The Papers of Henry H. Arnold, Library of Congress, , Washington, DC, author's emphasis.
[223] Arnold to Spaatz, 19 August 1942, author's emphasis.
[224] Major General C.A. Spaatz, Commanding General, Eighth Air Force to Brigadier General G.E. Stratemeyer, Chief of Staff, Commanding General, Army Air Forces, letter, 21 August 1942, Box 186, in The Papers of Henry H. Arnold, Library of Congress, Washington, DC.
[225] Major General C.A. Spaatz, Commanding General, Eighth Air Force, to Lieutenant General H.H. Arnold, Commanding General, Army Air Forces, War Department Message, 31 August 1942, Box 186, in The Papers of Henry H. Arnold, Library of Congress, Washington, DC.

airpower in a supporting role instead of a possible stand-alone, war-winning arm of the military on par with Eighth Air Force efforts in Europe. With this in mind, Arnold stood at a moral crossroads in Washington, DC. He knew the independence of the Air Force relied upon the type of warfare being waged in Europe, not the Pacific. For him, when Arnold made the prioritization of limited resources, the decision was simple.

Harmon represented a formidable obstacle in this scenario. As one of a handful of great Army Air Forces leaders in 1942, Harmon's observations, recommendations, and priorities carried significant meaning. The Navy recognized this and used it to its advantage in the great quest for more assets. As a commander in the Pacific, Harmon cared less about inter-service politics as long as the United States advanced the war against the Japanese. Writing to Brigadier General Laurence Kuter, a fellow former ACTS instructor and now the Deputy Chief of the Air Staff, Harmon said to "tell Gen Arnold it won't be long now before I am wearing 'bell bottom trousers' but nevertheless this is a job with a high degree of interest. Of course, it's a bit tough at times not to be operating one's bombers and to listen to a Navy chap talking about 'my B-17s,' but everything and anything goes as long as we lick the Jap."[226] To Arnold, that was but part of the picture. The Army Air Forces chief knew Harmon had obligations in the Pacific, but so too did Arnold have obligations in Washington, DC. The subordination of airpower to the Navy posed a great danger in his quest for Air Force independence. Under these ambiguous conditions, Arnold chose to visit the South Pacific

---

[226] Notes from Murray Green collection, *AAF Operates Under Navy Command in South Pacific – Sept 1942,* reference Major General M.F. Harmon to Brigadier General L.S. Kuter, letter, 11 September 1942, L/C Box 88, 8.59, The Murray Green Collection, US Air Force Academy Library, Colorado Springs, CO, author's emphasis.

firsthand and talk directly to Harmon and the other South Pacific leaders.

Figure 13: Harmon and Twining. Major General Millard F. Harmon, Jr confers with his air boss, Brigadier General Nathan F. Twining. Source: Millard F. Harmon, III. Picture in the author's collection.

Ghormley and the Battle on board the USS *Argonne*

> "I have to spill this to somebody, a little bit of what is on my mind, so I am afraid you will have to be the goat, but I hope you will burn this after it is read. It looks so to me that we are doing their job all over the world and the Government is not backing us up down here with what we need, why, I don't know."
>
> *VADM Ghormley to ADM Nimitz, September 7, 1942*

Admiral Ghormley was an unexpected pick as commander of all South Pacific forces, and proved to be one of Admiral King's "least fortunate choices."[227] Regarded as a highly intellectual man with vast experience, Ghormley "proved unequal to heading off military crises or dealing with them when they came."[228] Ghormley spent the previous few years serving in Europe on attaché duties and ran into Harmon in the spring of 1941 while the latter was with the Harriman Mission.[229] Ghormley's impressive resume lacked significant combat or operational planning experiences. His leadership style failed to inspire his subordinates, and his command approach confined him to the safety of his headquarters ship, the USS *Argonne*.[230] Ghormley rarely went ashore and almost never spent time with his senior Army commander Harmon. According to Twining, Ghormley once told Harmon, "my place is here by these dispatches, here's where I belong Miff."[231]

---

[227] E.B. Potter, *Nimitz* (Annapolis, MD: Naval Institute Press, 1976), 46 – 47.
[228] Potter, *Nimitz,* 47.
[229] General Henry Viccellio, interview by Dr. Murray Green, 13 May 1970, transcript, Note card 8.59, The Murray Green Collection, US Air Force Academy Library, Colorado Springs, CO.
[230] Potter, *Nimitz,* 196.
[231] Twining, interview, 3 November 1967.

When General Arnold arrived in theater and met Ghormley aboard the USS *Argonne* on September 23, he could immediately tell that the senior naval officers had "blood in their eye[s]."[232] Ghormley wasted no time imparting his own estimate of the situation on a man he felt had come to meddle in his operations. Twining remembered Ghormley told Arnold "he didn't' know what he was talking about. He was no dammed good; he wasn't supporting his forces."[233] In response, Arnold stated he intended to fact-find only, which seemed to cool temperatures at the meeting. Over the next few days, Arnold attempted to address many of the Navy's grievances and Harmon's concerns regarding the availability of aircraft and the priorities given to the South Pacific. While outwardly cooperative, privately, Arnold wasted little time before criticizing the entire South Pacific effort in his diaries.

First, Arnold wrote that the "Navy supply system onshore [was] a joke."[234] Furthermore, the "Navy did not give importance to either airports or gasoline," underscoring Harmon's judgment regarding the poor prioritization of runway equipment and material.[235] Second, Arnold agreed with Harmon and his staff that the "limitations of air operations" stemmed from a lack of "facilities and airports."[236] But this fact was lost on Ghormley, who deeply resented any criticism of his use of air assets. Arnold wrote that McCain wanted to go "whole hog for B-17's" while simultaneously misusing them for routine search missions more appropriate for Navy PBYs. Finally, Arnold judged the Navy's use of their own ships

---

[232] Huston, *America's Airpower Comes of Age*, 388.
[233] General Nathan F. Twining, interview by Dr. Murray Green, 2 January 1970, transcript, Box 9, Addendum 20, The Murray Green Collection, US Air Force Academy Library, Colorado Springs, CO.
[234] Huston, *America's Airpower Comes of Age*, 391.
[235] Huston, *America's Airpower Comes of Age*, 391.
[236] Huston, *America's Airpower Comes of Age*, 391.

as timid. The "Navy cannot handle land operations effectively. They are afraid to run ships into Guadalcanal and hold them until the things needed most... are unloaded."[237] Ultimately, Arnold felt the "Navy [did] not understand ground or air operations."[238]

On September 30, Arnold and his small staff departed the South Pacific Theater for the long journey home to Washington, DC. Following days of heated discussions and some major aircraft modifications, it appears only one contentious item was resolved: Harmon altered his opinion of the Airacobras and now found the P-39s tolerably suited to their South Pacific task. With the removal of four thirty-caliber machine guns, the P-39 lost 600 pounds and could finally reach Japanese bombers at altitude. Yet Harmon still disliked the export variant P-400 being flown at Guadalcanal, and in a meeting with Arnold, Nimitz, Ghormley, and Kenney, Harmon put Arnold on the spot for a squadron of P-38s.[239] Although Arnold held steadfast, P-38s did arrive in theater a few weeks later. It is unclear who released the P-38s, but a coincidental visit to Guadalcanal by then Undersecretary of the Navy James Forrestal holds clues. Apparently, upon seeing the conditions in the South Pacific and after spending time with Harmon and Twining, Forrestal returned to Washington, DC, and "had quite a battle."[240] A few days after Forrestal and Arnold's visits, the first P-38s arrived in theater.

Arnold's departure from the South Pacific did little to ease inter-service friction. In fact, if anything, Arnold's visit exacerbated

---

[237] Huston, *America's Airpower Comes of Age*, 392.
[238] Huston, *America's Airpower Comes of Age*, 401.

[239] "Notes on Conference held aboard U.S.S. *Argonne* at Noumea," 28 September 1942, Admiral's Letters – 1942, Series XIII, Early Records Collection, Operational Archives Branch, Naval Historical Center, Washington, DC, 23.

[240] Twining, interview, 3 November 1967.

tensions. Hap's legendary temper and his overt disdain for the Navy were readily apparent. During the first day of discussion on board the *Argonne*, Arnold attacked the senior Navy officers, accusing them of failing to fight. According to Twining, Arnold told the Navy officers, "they'd better start fighting the war instead of trying to get somebody else to fight the war for them."[241] Correspondingly, the Navy's dislike for Arnold culminated with his expulsion from the USS *Argonne* that afternoon.[242]

It fell to Harmon to mend fractured inter-service relations after his air boss left. He went to work immediately, outlining requirements for air forces and addressing the growing concerns for troop conditions on Guadalcanal. Harmon's loyalty to his chain of command in theater, in spite of clear shortcomings, paid great dividends in Nimitz and Ghormley's eyes. Miff's ability to operate effectively with joint partners made him a reliable colleague in the South Pacific Theater. But it came at a price. In a matter of weeks, Harmon found himself inside the inner ring of the Navy's trusted circle and outside of Arnold's for the next several months.

The War on the Ground

For the better part of thirty years, Miff Harmon had trained and succeeded as a pilot. Having flown combat missions over Mexico, Europe, and now the Pacific, he stood as one of the Air Force's most seasoned combat aviators. However, the Army played a trick on him when it ordered him to serve as the commanding general of all Army forces, air, and land, in the South Pacific. The nation needed Harmon to be a soldier as well as an airman.

---

[241] Twining, interview, 3 November 1967.
[242] Twining, interview, 2 January 1970.

By October 1942, the situation on Guadalcanal had worsened. The Japanese had reinforced the island garrison significantly. Henderson Field remained under constant attack while the pilots of the Cactus Air Force did their best to support the exhausted Marines and soldiers further inland. As friend and foe settled into an epic struggle at Guadalcanal, Admiral Ghormley planned the strategically irrelevant invasion of the neighboring island of Ndeni.

The invasion and capture of Ndeni had been a part of the initial campaign design for the Solomons; but with the fighting for Henderson Field entering a critical stage, Harmon was shocked that Ghormley held fast to Ndeni instead of reinforcing ongoing efforts at Guadalcanal. Writing to Ghormley on October 6, Harmon outlined his objections to the occupation of Ndeni. Harmon told Ghormley that "from a military viewpoint, the occupation of Ndini [sic] at this time" was a poor use of forces in the South Pacific.[243] Moreover, while the rationale for the occupation of Ndeni was valid before, efforts against that island represented a "diversion from the main effort and dispersion of force[s]."[244] Harmon was convinced that Guadalcanal hung in the balance, and he wrote the situation could not be considered anything but "continuingly critical."[245] He also stated that it was his "personal conviction that the Jap [was] capable of retaking Cactus-Ringbolt[246] and that he

[243] Major General M.F. Harmon, Commanding General, United States Army Forces in the South Pacific Area, to Vice Admiral R.L. Ghormley, Commander, South Pacific, letter, 6 October 1942, in Millard F. Harmon, Jr. Papers, 705.04A, IRIS No. 0251243, AFHRA.

[244] Harmon to Ghormley, 6 October 1942.

[245] Harmon to Ghormley, 6 October 1942.

[246] Ringbolt was the codename for Tulagi.

will do so in the near future unless it [was] materially strengthened."[247]

Harmon recommended to Ghormley eight distinct measures to stabilize the situation in the Solomons before conditions turned worse. Three of the most critical objectives included the "abandonment of the Ndeni operation," the "immediate re-enforcement of Cactus," and an "intensification... of naval surface action."[248] Most of Harmon's other suggestions focused on his familiar cry for supply, air action, and airfield construction. One recommendation for increased naval surface action rankled Ghormley. Harmon and Arnold had advocated for some time a more aggressive use of naval power in the South Solomons area. Ghormley, still reeling from the disaster at Savo Island, apparently answered, "I can't risk my ships."[249]

Ghormley met with Harmon to resolve these issues. After a lengthy discussion, Ghormley decided to continue preparations for the assault on Ndeni.[250] Harmon was able, however, to convince his boss of the growing threat to the forces on Guadalcanal and the immediate need to reinforce the island. Tropical diseases alone claimed substantial casualties, as Harmon predicted, with nearly 2,000 Marines requiring hospitalization in October alone.[251] Admiral Ghormley agreed, and two days later, he acquiesced to Harmon's pressure and ordered the 164th Infantry of the Americal Division to deploy to Guadalcanal.[252] Five days later, that unit

---

[247] Harmon to Ghormley, 6 October 1942.
[248] Harmon to Ghormley, 6 October 1942.
[249] Viccellio, interview, 13 May 1970.
[250] Miller, *Guadalcanal*, 141.
[251] Miller, *Guadalcanal: The First Offensive*, 141.
[252] Louis Morton, *United States Army in World War II, The War in the Pacific, Strategy and Command: The First Two Years* (1962; new imprint, Washington,

arrived at Lunga Point, where Major General Alexander Vandegrift, commander of the Marines ashore, immediately assigned them to perimeter defense of the besieged airfield.[253] Almost without delay, these new arrivals at Henderson Field found themselves under vicious attack. On the night of October 12 and into the next morning, the Japanese launched an intense air, ground, and naval bombardment of the American positions on Henderson Field. Harmon's warnings of a Japanese counterattack proved correct as US forces suffered the worst shelling of the entire campaign.[254] Without the new reinforcements, it is hard to imagine the Americans would have held the vital airstrip.

The following morning, Army Air Forces B-17s evacuated the shelled field while fighter squadrons scraped together their remaining machines. In a remarkable display of courage, men of the Cactus Air Force continued to operate, thwarting further Japanese resupply efforts, although they could only muster a fraction of the desired sorties. By October 16, both Ghormley and Harmon feared the worst. Ghormley "warned Admiral Nimitz that the Japanese effort appeared to be 'all out.'"[255] Harmon sent several messages back to General Marshall in Washington, DC warning the situation on Guadalcanal was grave. "It is my opinion," he wrote in one dispatch, "position Cactus untenable without more naval surface support. Ghormley has not yet announced definite line of action he proposes pursue in light [of the] developments [of

---

DC: Center of Military History, 2000), 342. Samuel B. Griffith, author of "The Battle for Guadalcanal," calls Harmon's memo to Ghormley, "a decisive document in the history of the Guadalcanal campaign," (Griffith, Samuel B., II. The *Battle for Guadalcanal.* Philadelphia: J.B. Lippincott Co., 1963, 142).

253 Morton, *Strategy and Command*, 342.

254 Miller, *Guadalcanal*, 149.

255 Miller, *Guadalcanal*, 152.

the] past week."[256] In this message, he again requested more air and ground reinforcements.

Fortunately, the Japanese forces on Guadalcanal failed to synchronize their air and naval action with aggressive infantry attacks against American positions. Skillful work by exhausted Marines and fresh Army troops was able to stave off waves of enemy assaults. By late October, the 1st Marine Division reported an estimated 2,200 enemy soldiers killed in action. The soldiers of the 164th Infantry survived their first enemy action under grueling circumstances. General Vandegrift stated that the fortuitous arrival of the 164th Infantry, because of Harmon's perseverance, prevented any "serious penetration of the [American] position and, by reinforcing the [Marines], made possible the repulse of continued enemy attacks."[257]

Prior to the final ground assaults in late October, Admiral Nimitz had seen enough. The thrashing of Savo Island, combined with the tenuous situation on Guadalcanal, led Nimitz to search for a new leader. On the evening of October 15, Nimitz convened a special meeting with the members of his staff who had traveled to the South Pacific and were familiar with the events. Nimitz polled the officers regarding Ghormley's leadership, and every single officer present "expressed the opinion that [Ghormley] did not have the required qualities" for command and the entire atmosphere of his headquarters was "intolerable."[258] Every officer told Nimitz to relieve Ghormley, and after conferring with Admiral King in

---

[256] Major General M.F. Harmon, Commanding General, United States Army Forces in the South Pacific Area, to General G.C. Marshall, Chief of Staff, War Department, letter, 17 October 1942, Box 187, in The Papers of Henry H. Arnold, Library of Congress, Washington, DC.
[257] Miller, *Guadalcanal*, 166.
[258] Potter, *Nimitz,* 196.

Washington, DC, he acted swiftly. In a note to his wife, Nimitz expressed regret for relieving his friend but believed "the interests of the nation transcend private interests."[259]

Bull Halsey

> "I have about reached the conclusion that the yellow bastards have been playing us for suckers."[260]
>
> *Halsey to Nimitz, October 31, 1942*

---

[259] Potter, *Nimitz,* 197.

[260] By modern standards, professional communication between senior leaders during World War II, many of which are quoted in the following chapters, would offend most readers. The reality of the situation, however, is that all players in World War II, and in most other conflicts as well, the killing of fellow humans sometimes requires one to dehumanize the other. Evan Thomas wrote in "Sea of Thunder," on January 7, 2007 that: "To twenty-first-century ears, Halsey sounds like a racist monster or a sadist. In his own time, however, he was regarded by the public as a war hero, a little outspoken, too crude perhaps, but refreshingly blunt about the true nature of the enemy and the hard job ahead. In the wartime America of the 1940s, Halsey's attitude was unexceptional. Americans routinely referred to the Japanese as "Japs" and "Nips," and often as animals or insects of some kind (most commonly, monkeys, baboons, gorillas, dogs, mice, rats, vipers and rattlesnakes, and cockroaches). The Japanese were just as bigoted. They depicted Americans and other Westerners as reptiles, worms, insects (rendered in cartoons with the faces of Franklin Roosevelt and Winston Churchill), frogs, octopuses, beached whales, and stray dogs. Dehumanizing the enemy to make it easier to kill them is an ancient practice between warring nations, but rarely has it been practiced with more depraved creativity than in the Pacific War." Truth demands quoting the leaders as they wrote it in that time.

Figure 14: Halsey and Harmon. Source: Louis Morton, United States Army in World War II, The War in the Pacific, Strategy and Command: The First Two Years (1962; new imprint, Washington, DC: Center of Military History, 2000), 357.

Miff Harmon wrote to Hap Arnold on October 20 with a situation update on Guadalcanal. Harmon felt the circumstances at "Cactus [remained] a most disturbing question."[261] For weeks, Harmon had lobbied Ghormley for an intensification of naval

[261] Major General M.F. Harmon, Commanding General, United States Army Forces in the South Pacific Area, to General H.H. Arnold, Commanding General, Army Air Forces, letter, 20 October 1942, in Millard F. Harmon, Jr. Papers, 705.161, IRIS No. 00251257, AFHRA.

surface support to stymie Tokyo Express reinforcements and intermittent shelling from the sea. Harmon told Arnold that "if our surface forces can stop the Jap freedom of action, particularly at night," and if the Americans could stabilize operations at Henderson Field, there was a chance they could "pull the fat out of the fire."[262] The only optimism in his letter was the report of new leadership in the South Pacific. "Halsey relieved Ghormley today. Perhaps there will be a difference in method or intensity of surface force action."[263]

Halsey's first action was to listen. On his first day of duty, Halsey listened to Ghormley lay out the ground situation. After only a few minutes, Halsey realized that neither Ghormley nor this staff "could give him a firsthand description of the situation."[264] Ghormley and his staff had been "too bogged down with paperwork to leave the *Argonne*," a habit Hap Arnold recognized during his September visit.[265] Halsey called a meeting with his senior leaders, including Vandegrift and Harmon. Vandegrift explained the deplorable situation outlining the toll taken by combat losses and ravages of disease, and stated he needed more support if he was to hold out. Halsey heard this and replied, "I promise to get you everything I have."[266]

Like Harmon's arrival in theater in July, the Navy had thrown Halsey into a developed situation and asked for urgent miracles. Halsey reported to Nimitz that he "took over a strange job with a strange staff" and had to begin "throwing punches almost

---

[262] Harmon to Arnold, 20 October 1942.
[263] Harmon to Arnold, 20 October 1942.
[264] Potter, *Nimitz,* 198.
[265] Potter, *Nimitz,* 198.
[266] Potter, *Nimitz,* 199.

immediately."[267] One of Halsey's first actions was to get off the *Argonne* and seek a building large enough to hold the staff of his subordinate components. Halsey also noted the troubling supply situation and began to move huge tank farms closer to the area of operations. After a brief survey of the tactical situation, he ordered drastic changes in the manner in which naval surface forces responded to enemy shipping. Aggressive submarine operations began to pay dividends against the nightly Tokyo Express ships. Asking Nimitz for "anything and everything that will float, can listen, and drop depth charges," Halsey stated that he intended to give the "sharks some damn fine monkey meat to eat."[268] Upon Halsey's assumption of command, offensive action on the part of the Americans "changed overnight."[269]

Halsey's aggressiveness was tonic to the Solomons situation. On November 1, Harmon wrote to Marshall that morale with the forces was improving as fast as the situation on Guadalcanal. "The picture has changed materially," Harmon wrote.[270] "I feel that the Jap can win now in the Solomons only by bold, aggressive action of heavily superior forces." Harmon further commented on the drastic change in leadership, "Halsey has shown aggressiveness and ingenuity. All heads are high here and will so remain."[271]

---

[267] Vice Admiral William F. Halsey, Commander, South Pacific, to Admiral Chester W. Nimitz, Commander in Chief, Pacific, letter, 31 October 1942, Admiral Nimitz Collection, Admiral's Letters – 1942, Series XIII, Early Records Collection, Operational Archives Branch, Naval Historical Center, Washington, DC.

[268] Halsey to Nimitz, 31 October 1942.

[269] Twining, interview, 2 January 1970.

[270] Major General M.F. Harmon, Commanding General, United States Army Forces in the South Pacific Area, to General G.C. Marshall, Chief of Staff, War Department, letter, 1 November 1942, courtesy Helen Harmon Nazzaro personal collection, in the author's collection.

[271] Harmon to Marshall, 1 November 1942.

Air operations increased as well, but high-altitude bombing was not producing the desired results. On one mission, aircraft dropped eighty-eight bombs and scored only two hits.[272] Halsey and Harmon conferred over these issues on November 6, and later that day, Halsey wrote to Nimitz that he "had a very free chat with Harmon on the subject of poor hitting by B-17's."[273] Halsey stated Harmon "knows that the only way to do so is to bring them down."[274] Harmon ordered new crews to train on skip bombing tactics and by December, the synergistic effects of aggressive naval surface action with improvements in Harmon's bombers all but "isolated the Japanese on Guadalcanal. The Tokyo Express could slip through on occasion, but the island's air forces limited its trips."[275]

Harmon's ingenuity, too, was evident in his response to this challenge. Harmon provided improved counter-sea efforts by implementing new tactics with his medium bomber forces. During his long journey from San Francisco in July, Harmon participated in several discussions with George Kenney regarding the feasibility of 'skip bombing' ships at low altitude. Kenney conducted initial skip bombing tests in July using Harmon's Fijian-based B-26s from Nandi.[276] Later, Harmon proposed skip bombing tactics using his own B-26s against the Tokyo Express. McCain had previously written about this development, saying the answer to Japanese

---

[272] Vice Admiral William F. Halsey, Commander, South Pacific, to Admiral Chester W. Nimitz, Commander in Chief, Pacific, letter, 6 November 1942, Admiral Nimitz Collection, Admiral's Letters – 1942, Series XIII, Early Records Collection, Operational Archives Branch, Naval Historical Center, Washington, DC., 6.

[273] Halsey to Nimitz, 6 November 1942, 6.

[274] Halsey to Nimitz, 6 November 1942, 6.

[275] Miller, *Guadalcanal*, 221.

[276] George Kenney, *General Kenney Reports* (New York: Duell, Sloan and Pearce, 1949), 22.

surface shipping seems "to be the low altitude skip bombing method now being tried out under General Harmon."[277]

While the air and sea situation was improving, the ground situation remained a challenge. During this period, Miff took the opportunity to readdress the issue of the temporarily postponed Ndeni operation. After making his case, Halsey accepted his advice and canceled the operation. Halsey revoked the 147th Infantry's orders for Ndeni and redirected them to Guadalcanal as much-needed reinforcements.[278] With the Japanese navy forced back on its heels and the Cactus Air Force beginning to reconstitute, the majority of the remaining combat operations fell to the ground forces on the island.

Much of the struggle had weighed on the 1st Marine Division, who had fought continuously since landing on Lunga Point in the very beginning. Heat, disease, and combat casualties had taken their toll, and as early as November 3, "Halsey had wished to relieve the worn-out division."[279] On the same day, Harmon reiterated a request to Marshall for the 25th Infantry Division, then in Hawaii in a defensive role. Major General J. Lawton Collins commanded the 'Tropic Lightning Division,' and by early December, in accordance with Harmon's requests, the unit sailed for Guadalcanal.

In the meantime, Halsey told Harmon to choose General Vandegrift's replacement as the senior man on Guadalcanal. Harmon picked Major General Alexander 'Sandy' Patch of the

---

[277] Rear Admiral John S. McCain, Commander, Air, South Pacific, to Rear Admiral Aubrey W. Fitch and Major General Millard F. Harmon, Jr., Commanding General, United States Army Forces in the South Pacific Area, letter, 19 September 1942, in Millard F. Harmon Papers, 705.161, AFHRA.

[278] Miller, *Guadalcanal*, 174.

[279] Miller, *Guadalcanal*, 212.

Americal Division on Noumea and immediately directed him to control all "tactical operations on Guadalcanal."[280] On December 8, the Army had assumed complete responsibility, and by the next day, units of the 1st Marines began to leave Guadalcanal. The remainder of the Americal Division joined Patch on Guadalcanal, who, after a quick survey of his forces, determined American troop strength was dangerously inadequate. The fresh troops of the under-strength Americal Division and the battle-fatigued 1st Marines, who still remained on the island, were insufficient to hold the objectives on Guadalcanal and prevent further enemy advances. Experienced troops remaining on Cactus were combat-weary and wrought with Malaria. While American troop strength hovered at a perilously low level, Halsey and Harmon both noted increasing enemy infiltration, and warned their superiors of what may be a final thrust by the enemy. "It appears to us as if something may be brewing, and, counting on that, we have gotten our available forces to sea, waiting for a chance to strike," Halsey told Nimitz on December 8.[281] With an impending counterattack by the enemy, and weakened friendly forces on the island, Harmon attempted a risky reinforcement operation.

Reinforcements Arrive

Normally, units arriving in the South Pacific Theater stopped in Noumea, New Caledonia, and prepared for the final leg of the journey to Guadalcanal. Noumea was the only modern port in the area capable of handling large ships, while Guadalcanal lacked such

---

[280] Miller, *Guadalcanal*, 213.
[281] Vice Admiral William F. Halsey, Commander, South Pacific, to Admiral Chester W. Nimitz, Commander in Chief, Pacific, letter, 8 December 1942, Admiral Nimitz Collection, Admiral's Letters – 1942, Series XIII, Early Records Collection, Operational Archives Branch, Naval Historical Center, Washington, DC.

amenities and still posed the threat of enemy action. The 'Tropic Lightning' division was enroute to Noumea for transshipment when Harmon redirected it to Guadalcanal to shave a few days off the itinerary. The "tactical situation and relief of First [Marine Division] dictates this procedure," Harmon wrote in a message to General Marshall in Washington, DC, even though the movement directly to Guadalcanal was perilous.[282] "Transshipment [sic] [in] Noumea would seriously interfere with and delay" the reinforcement of troops ashore and jeopardize shipping operations around the area.[283] Concerned with the potentially catastrophic consequences of failure, Marshall responded on December 8. "I do not, repeat, not propose to question your decision as to tactical utilization of forces under your command but want you to be fully informed as to the status of loading of 25th Division units in view of conditions inherent to the debarkation of such forces in an area where security is questionable and port facilities practically nonexistent. Acknowledge receipt this radio."[284] Harmon, knowledgeable of the serious risks involved, acknowledged Marshall's message and waited pensively for the 25th Infantry to arrive. Under the cover of intense air and sea cover, the 25th Infantry Division arrived on Guadalcanal on January 4, 1943, with no losses. Harmon's gamble paid off and gave Patch the three divisions necessary to hold Guadalcanal and fight further Japanese advances. In light of this

---

[282] Major General M.F. Harmon, Commanding General, United States Army Forces in the South Pacific Area, to General G.C. Marshall, Chief of Staff, War Department, message, 6 December 1942, 750.161-1, IRIS No. 00260973, AFHRA.

[283] Harmon to Marshall, 6 December 1942.

[284] General G.C. Marshall, Chief of Staff, War Department, to Major General M.F. Harmon, Commanding General, United States Army Forces in the South Pacific Area, message, 8 December 1942, 750.161-1, IRIS No. 00260973, AFHRA.

improved troop strength, Harmon closed the 'Cactus Corps' and activated the Fourteenth Corps with Patch in command.

Figure 15: Harmon and Patch. Ca. early 1943. Source: Millard F. Harmon, III. Picture in the author's collection.

During this same period, with American troop strength rising, Halsey and Harmon launched a prelude attack that would culminate in a larger operation upon arrival of the 25th Infantry Division. The objective was the capture of Mount Austen, a 1,500-foot rise that dominated the area around Henderson Field. Ranging only six miles from the airstrip, Austen stood as a strategic high ground that Japanese forces could use to rain artillery shells down on the Americans. In early December, Admiral Halsey ordered Harmon to "eliminate all Japanese forces on the island," thereby giving him, for the first time and, although temporarily, direct control over tactical operations on the island.[285]

[285] Miller, *Guadalcanal*, 232.

Harmon immediately flew to Guadalcanal to review and approve Patch's plan of action. An initial probing operation in mid-December found light resistance on Mount Austen, causing the Americans to believe that the Japanese had abandoned their positions. By the third week of December, after fighting for nearly six days, the Americans realized their initial estimations were grossly overoptimistic. What started as a preliminary action as part of a larger operation, the assault quickly became a massive battle encompassing the majority of the eastern side of the island. Battles raged at Galloping Horse, Kokumbona, the Sea Horse, and Gifu until the Americans forced the Japanese off Guadalcanal in early February.

Air support during this period was heroic. Operating under the difficult pressures found in the South Pacific, the joint efforts of the Army, Navy, and Marines served as a powerful force multiplier. P-39s "contributed in large measure to the success of the Guadalcanal Campaign through [the] employment of bombs, machine gun, and cannon fire, destroying shipping and small barges transporting troops, and in direct support of ground operations."[286] In one battle, P-39s accounted for 170 of 900 total Japanese soldiers killed.[287] Harmon attributed the impressive results by the less-than-optimum P-39s to the courageous fighter pilots of those units.

The B-17s based in Espiritu Santo also proved themselves effective combat weapons.[288] The Flying Fortresses performed well against all ground targets but experienced setbacks in the air against the Japanese Zeros and frontal strafing attacks. Responding

---

[286] Harmon, *Army in the South Pacific*, 14.
[287] Harmon, *Army in the South Pacific*, 14.
[288] Craven and Cate, *The Pacific – Guadalcanal to Saipan*, 62.

to this enemy action, Harmon requested defensive modifications to his B-17s. The Army installed two fifty-caliber nose guns and another in the radio area.[289] Almost immediately, the Fortresses improved their defensive record against the Zero.

As his air component continued to grow, Harmon again addressed the Navy's operational control over Army aircraft. In an attempt to recapture direct influence over the aircraft, Harmon argued for the creation of a new organization to manage South Pacific air forces. Arnold and Marshall agreed with Harmon, and on December 5, Marshall ordered him to create the Thirteenth Air Force.[290] Harmon did so and appointed his best air commander, Brigadier General Nathan Twining, to be its first commander.

Figure 16: Harmon and Twining. Along with Harmon's daughter Helen in the United States, ca 1943. Source: Helen Harmon Nazzaro. Picture in the author's collection.

---

[289] Craven and Cate, *The Pacific – Guadalcanal to Saipan,* 62.
[290] Craven and Cate, *The Pacific – Guadalcanal to Saipan,* 71.

Harmon ordered the Thirteenth Air Force to establish its headquarters on Espiritu Santo, near Rear Admiral Aubrey Fitch's headquarters, who had replaced Admiral McCain as COMAIRSOLS. Harmon believed that if the Thirteenth Air Force was to be effective, it needed to be in close proximity with the other air headquarters.[291] Although the Navy still had operational control of Army Air Forces planes, the creation of the Thirteenth Air Force was a step in the right direction, because it gave Army air commanders the capability to effectively organize, supervise and train their air forces. Previously, Harmon organized subordinate air units by island commands, and the Navy parceled those units out as they saw fit. Now, the Navy could coordinate with a single Army air commander, ensuring a modicum of Army unity of command. Within Twining's organization, Col Dean Strother commanded all fighter operations, and Col Harlan McCormick led bomber operations.[292]

Lessons from Cactus

As major combat operations on Guadalcanal ebbed, the Americans made plans for further advances up the Solomons chain. This time, Harmon was able to participate extensively during the genesis of the operational plans. He brought with him a number of insights from his time fighting for Guadalcanal. Harmon's late introduction to a chaotic organization had hamstrung his efforts against the Japanese until it was almost too late. Harmon learned from this experience, as he had numerous times in his career, that there was no substitute for detailed, joint planning prior to major combat operations. Harmon also learned that the 'war' in

---

[291] Craven and Cate, *The Pacific – Guadalcanal to Saipan,* 72.
[292] Craven and Cate, *The Pacific – Guadalcanal to Saipan,* 73.

Washington, DC had direct consequences on the actions in the field, a truth he loathed. Hap Arnold's quest for an independent Air Force, by way of the defeat of industrial Germany, meant the Pacific war was not an Air Force war but a Navy war. As such, Arnold sent what little he could to help Harmon beat the Japanese. Twining later reflected on this, stating Arnold "wasn't going to give the Air Force outfit [in the South Pacific] a dammed thing... [the Navy] was supposed to run it. He had a war in Europe and wasn't going to give them a thing."[293] With little options available to him, Harmon scraped together the best aircraft he had and argued for more reinforcements.

Harmon did not always get what he wanted. His frequent requests for supplies, in the middle of horrible fighting on Guadalcanal, often went unfilled. Admiral Ghormley was not much help because his lack of leadership and fear of defeat made aggressive action nearly impossible. During this period, Harmon used his strong sense of service and unwavering loyalty to navigate the South Pacific organizational quagmire. He was able to construct strong working relationships with the senior naval officers who carried Harmon's message to the highest levels, ultimately delivering the replacements desperately needed. Even after Arnold's visit, one that nearly destroyed the good relationships Miff had built, the Navy continued to rely on Harmon's expertise.

On February 3, 1943, Millard F. Harmon, Jr. received his long overdue promotion to Lieutenant General in the United States Army. During the preceding seven months, Harmon served in the South Pacific as a two-star general, while Kenney, the air commander in the Southwest Pacific, had been a three-star general for nearly a year. It is unclear if the Army Air Forces delayed

[293] Twining, interview, 2 January 1970.

Harmon's promotion, but it is clear that Admiral Halsey pushed for it through Admiral Nimitz. In fact, Admiral Halsey not only officiated at Harmon's promotion but also gave him his personal three-star insignia for his uniform.[294]

[294] Unknown newspaper clipping from Helen Harmon Nazzaro collection dated 17 February 1943, "Harmon gets Promotion."

Chapter Eight: Forward Through the South Pacific

> "The commander, I believe, who is principally responsible for the cooperation, assistance and help that has been 100 percent every time we have called on him is your General Harmon."
>
> *Admiral W.F. 'Bull' Halsey, February 17, 1943*

> "You have been doing a grand job and we are all proud of you."
>
> *President Franklin D. Roosevelt to Harmon, August 15, 1943*

In early 1943, supplies remained in short supply for the soldiers of the South Pacific, forcing Harmon's staff to take drastic measures in an effort to conserve critical resources. While not official policy, headquarters decided only two bullets should be allotted to kill one Japanese soldier. In a flurry of memos and heated letters between Harmon's office and Major General J. Lawton Collins, officers uncovered a careless use of ammunition.

> *SUBJECT: EXCESS EXPENDITURE OF AMMUNITION*
>
> *1. It has come to the attention of this headquarters, unofficially, that one of your commanders, Major Gen. Joseph L. Collins, personally expended eight rounds of .30-caliber ammunition for a net return of*

> *only one Jap sniper. This is considered an excessive expenditure of ammunition by at least six rounds, particularly in view of General Collins' previous record as an expert rifleman. Furthermore, it is understood that considerable damage to a coconut tree resulted from his firing. This may later develop into a claim against the government.*[295]

Collins wasted no time replying to Harmon's staff, blaming the event on his "old age, failing eyesight, and buck fever." "Pas bon!"[296]* Harmon jokingly replied. "How are my brigadiers with M1 rifles?"[297]

Figure 17: USAFISPA Staff – 1943. Major General Millard F. Harmon, Jr. (center), Brigadier General Twining (right of Harmon). Source: Millard F. Harmon, III. Picture in the author's collection.

---

[295] "8 Shots 'Per Jap' Shame a General: Censured for Wasting Bullets on Guadalcanal. He Blames 'Eyesight and Buck Fever.'" *New York Times,* 23 March 1943.

[296] *Not Good!*

[297] "8 Shots 'Per Jap' Shame a General: Censured for Wasting Bullets on Guadalcanal. He Blames 'Eyesight and Buck Fever.'" *New York Times,* 23 March 1943.

Instances of levity around the headquarters were critical, especially as the men of the South Pacific completed their seventh month of sustained combat operations. With clean-up work ongoing at Guadalcanal, Harmon and Halsey weighed their next options. Japanese strength in the Solomons had taken a substantial blow with the loss of Guadalcanal. However, a sizeable garrison remained at Rabaul, with a number of smaller fortifications between it and Guadalcanal. With naval carrier strength still lower than necessary, the two leaders knew that the range of the land-based fighter aircraft would ultimately determine the next objective.[298]

Prior to the fall of Guadalcanal on February 8, General Douglas MacArthur and the South Pacific commanders determined their next mission would be the reduction of Rabaul. However, the method by which Allied forces should accomplish this objective was in dispute. Bomber operations and air superiority were critical for the assault on Rabaul. These meant new airbases were necessary on nearby Bougainville, which in turn mandated the occupation of either New Georgia or the Russells. MacArthur felt the South Pacific forces could bypass New Georgia and attack Bougainville from the Russells alone.[299] Harmon believed otherwise and advocated an invasion of the Russells, followed by operations to take New Georgia. This was necessary to allow sufficient forces to be prepared for a follow-on assault of Bougainville. Halsey agreed with Harmon and, using their collective experience from Guadalcanal, developed plans to take the Russell Islands and New Georgia while

---

[298] Harmon, *Army in the South Pacific*, 7.

[299] Louis Morton, *United States Army in World War II, The War in the Pacific, Strategy and Command: The First Two Years* (1962; new imprint, Washington, DC: Center of Military History, 2000), 401.

working to ensure adequate supplies were ready for both operations.[300]

Harmon relinquished operational control of tactical land forces on Guadalcanal to Patch, later replaced by Major General Oscar Griswold of the XIV Corps, and began preparations for the invasion of the Russell islands.[301] On February 21, the 43rd Infantry Division, under the command of Major General John Hester, invaded the Russells in an operation codenamed CLEANSLATE.[302] Hester met little Japanese resistance, and within three weeks, nearly 16,000 men were ashore, working on a new airfield, torpedo boat, and landing craft bases and finalizing preparations for the New Georgia effort.[303] On April 15, the airfield was complete and ready to support subsequent operations against New Georgia. The overwhelming success of the timely completion of the Russells airfield was due to the prioritization of airfield equipment in the early stages, a lesson learned by Harmon during Guadalcanal.

With the airfield complete, Halsey accomplished his objective of securing a permanent base within reach of the major Japanese airstrip at Munda Point on New Georgia.[304] The New Georgia operation was expected to be much more difficult than what Harmon dubbed division "amphibious training" in the Russells.[305]

---

[300] Louis Morton, *Strategy and Command*, 505.
[301] Harmon, *Army in the South Pacific*, 7.
[302] John Miller, Jr. *United States Army in World War II, The War in the Pacific, Guadalcanal: The First Offensive* (Washington, DC: Department of the Army, 1949), 354-356.
[303] Miller, *Guadalcanal*, 351.
[304] Fleet Admiral William F. Halsey and Lieutenant Commander J. Bryan III, *Admiral Halsey's Story* (New York, NY: Whittlesey House, 1947), 153.
[305] Harmon, *Army in the South Pacific*, 7.

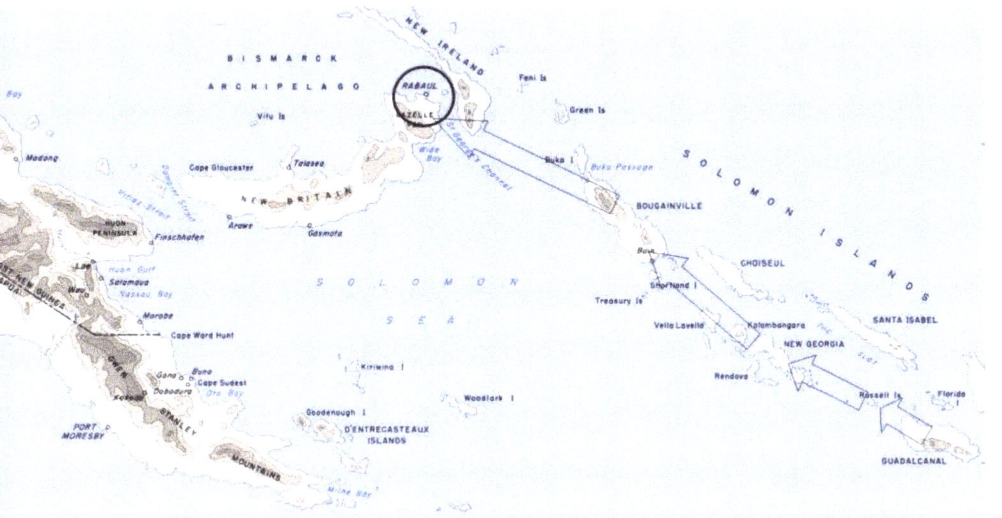

Figure 18: SOPAC's Advance through the Solomons. Source: Map 3 from John Miller, Jr., United States Army in World War II, The War in the Pacific, CARTWHEEL: The Reduction of Rabaul (Washington, DC: Center of Military History, 1959), 23. Author's additional graphics.

The Japanese forces on New Georgia numbered several thousand, and the airfield at Munda was active with multiple fighter aircraft. This airfield was Harmon's target due to its prime location on the northwest side of the island, putting it within striking distance of Rabaul and the great quantity of coral that was available for runway repair and additional construction.[306] In preparation for the landing of the 43rd Division, the combined air forces of the South Pacific began a systematic pounding of both Munda airfield and Vila airfield on nearby Kolombangara Island.[307] Within a few days, the Japanese abandoned major positions on the island, paving the way for Major General Hester and his forces.

Command arraignments for the New Georgia campaign were muddled, a common trend in the Pacific Theater. Command

[306] Harmon, *Army in the South Pacific*, 7.
[307] Harmon, *Army in the South Pacific*, 7.

responsibility for the entire invasion fell to Rear Admiral Richmond Turner, while the 43rd Division Commander, Major General Hester, maintained command of land forces. Halsey, as was his pattern through the SOPAC campaign, maintained overall command and exercised direct control of all naval forces. Air operations, including Navy, Marine, Army, and New Zealand assets, went to Admiral Fitch, who consulted with the Thirteenth Air Force commander, Major General Twining.[308] Harmon remained in his advisory role to Halsey and ensured all Army forces received the supplies and training necessary. Surveying this arrangement, Harmon recognized early on that Turner would be unable to monitor ground operations efficiently, yet Turner was unwilling to relinquish that authority to a more capable commander.[309] At the same time, General Hester's dual responsibilities as division commander and New Georgian operations commander worried Harmon. Harmon frequently stressed the principle of unity of

---

[308] Prior to the New Georgia operation, Nathan Twining, Glen C. Jamison and thirteen other men ditched in the South Pacific waters near Guadalcanal. The B-17 they were on ran out of fuel, crashed in the ocean and sank within minutes. Equipped with limited supplies, the men lashed their two life rafts together and divided the canteen and a half of water and single chocolate bar between themselves. Harmon learned of the accident and personally led airborne search missions on January 28 and 30, 1943. On January 29, Harmon directed the operation from his headquarters. After five days and six nights, Harmon decided to suspend the search operations, convinced his men were lost. However, on that day, a Navy PBY aircraft spotted the life rafts and rescued the stranded crewmembers. During their ordeal, men on the rafts would occasionally jump into the water to cool off and stretch their legs, only to be chased back into the rafts by sharks. Additionally, Twining provided food when he shot an Albatross out of the sky with his .45 caliber pistol. The men ate the bird raw including the squid in the bird's stomach. After a few days of medical attention and rest, Twining and the others went to work planning the invasion of the Russells and New Georgia with Harmon. (See "Twining Sea Rescue," 168.7109-3, IRIS No. 1028001, AFHRA)

[309] Louis Morton, *Strategy and Command*, 511.

command throughout his South Pacific experience, and the New Georgian operation was in direct violation of this practice.[310] In light of this potential pitfall, Harmon notified Major General Griswold on Guadalcanal to be prepared to move forward to New Georgia if a crisis developed.

Attacked on Board the *McCawley*

On June 30, Harmon and Turner, both aboard the USS *McCawley* just offshore, watched Major General Hester invade Rendova Island in the New Georgian group with his 43rd Division and two Marine Raider Battalions. As operations continued, Japanese torpedo bombers arrived in the landing area. Several enemy aircraft swooped down on the *McCawley*, forcing the men on board to respond with intense anti-aircraft fire. *McCawley*'s skilled sailors destroyed four Japanese aircraft during the attack, yet many survived, and a few delivered their deadly payloads. Several torpedoes struck the *McCawley*; one in particular crippled the engine room, killing fifteen sailors. The command ship was immobilized, and for fear of further Japanese attacks on the helpless vessel, Turner and Harmon evacuated to shore.[311]

---

[310] Louis Morton, *Strategy and Command*, 511.

[311] This entire paragraph is a compilation of various sources. Many newspaper clippings in the personal collection of Helen Harmon Nazzaro detail the fact that Japanese torpedo aircraft sunk Harmon and Turner's landing craft during the invasion of Rendova in the New Georgia group. Those newspaper clippings do not have dates or newspaper titles. Strategy and Command: The First Two Years by Louis Morton mentions the loss of the flagship during the invasion on page 507. The Dictionary of American Naval Fighting Ships describes the events of 30 June 1943 on board the *McCawley*. The website for the DANFS can be located at http://www.history.navy.mil/danfs/m7/mccawley-ii.htm (accessed 15 April 2007).

Once ashore, Harmon's initial impressions of Operation TOENAILS were favorable, and he credited Hester with this success. Shortly thereafter, on July 2, South Pacific forces landed on New Georgia proper along the southern coast near Munda Point. By July 5, however, Harmon began to have serious misgivings regarding the pace of operations and Hester's ability to manage his own division in addition to the combat operations on New Georgia. Over the next several days, Harmon and Turner were in "violent disagreement" regarding the remedy for New Georgia. Each man offered dissimilar solutions.[312] Harmon advocated Griswold move from Guadalcanal to Munda following its capture, and take responsibility for the occupation forces at the airfield. Harmon still supported Hester as the commander of the 43rd Division but told Halsey that portions of the XIV Corps staff should also move forward to augment Hester's understaffed unit. Turner wholly disagreed with this proposition, and the two officers went to Halsey on July 6 for a resolution. Meeting with Halsey, Turner expressed that the injection of Griswold would "deal a severe blow to the morale of the troops" under Hester's current command.[313] Halsey disagreed.

Over the next few days and after several intermediate iterations, Hester was relieved of command of New Georgian occupation forces and replaced by Griswold according to Harmon's recommendations. Halsey also removed Admiral Turner as the overall commander and reassigned him to the Central Pacific Theater, a move already under consideration prior to the commencement of operations on New Georgia. Finally, on July 13, after further questions regarding the effectiveness of ground

---

[312] Louis Morton, *Strategy and Command*, 509.
[313] Louis Morton, *Strategy and Command*, 509.

forces ashore, Halsey directed Harmon to "assume full charge of and responsibility for ground operations in New Georgia," with Griswold leading tactical operations.[314] The decision to support Harmon was no small matter. Harmon recommended the removal of an Army general officer with decades of infantry experience. The relief of General Hester drew the immediate attention of Admiral Nimitz in Hawaii, who asked Halsey for an explanation.[315] Halsey responded saying Hester "was traveling on his nerve" and needed rest.[316] Based upon Harmon's recommendations, Halsey installed Griswold as commander of New Georgian occupation forces, leaving Hester in control of his division only. For a moment, this leadership shake-up streamlined command arraignments, with Harmon responsible for all of New Georgia, reporting directly to Halsey. Unfortunately, it did not solve many problems with the Japanese.

Fighting in New Georgia was extremely difficult. The summer heat and fetid conditions continued to take their toll as the Americans struggled in a dense jungle environment. Enemy resistance was stiff, stalling the Allied advance by the third week of July. In response to the slow pace of movement, Harmon ordered fresh reinforcements to the scene as Griswold, under Harmon's

---

[314] Harmon, *Army in the South Pacific*, 8.
[315] Admiral Chester W. Nimitz, Commander in Chief, Pacific, to Vice Admiral William F. Halsey, Commander, South Pacific, letter, 8 August 1943, Admiral's Letters – 1942, Series XIII, Early Records Collection, Operational Archives Branch, Naval Historical Center, Washington, DC.
[316] Vice Admiral William F. Halsey, Commander, South Pacific, to Admiral Chester W. Nimitz, Commander in Chief, Pacific, letter, 19 August 1943, Admiral Nimitz Collection, Admiral's Letters – 1942, Series XIII, Early Records Collection, Operational Archives Branch, Naval Historical Center, Washington, DC.

orders, prepared to launch a new offensive against Munda airfield.[317]

On July 25, the ferocious fighting resumed as the 43rd Division made its final assault against fortified Japanese positions around Munda airfield. Progress stalled again, and after a few days, Harmon completely relieved Hester of command of the 43rd Division and installed Brigadier General John Hodge as commander. Harmon felt Hester "had lost too much sap, and [was] also out of contact with his own outfit."[318] As a result, Harmon intended to talk to Hester and send him back to the headquarters.[319] After a much-needed rest, and based upon how "he carries his tail," Harmon felt Hester could regain his command.[320]

Coincidentally, as Hodge took command, Japanese forces began a withdrawal from the Munda area, and by August 1, Harmon reported to Halsey that the "fight would be over in time for tea tomorrow."[321] On August 4, Harmon affirmed it was "open season on Nips," and by the next afternoon, the Americans captured Munda airfield.[322] For the next three weeks, forces under Harmon's command conducted "mopping up operations," and on August 25, the campaign for New Georgia was over.[323]

---

[317] Louis Morton, *Strategy and Command,* 511.
[318] Lieutenant General M.F. Harmon, Jr., Commanding General, United States Army Forces in the South Pacific Area, memorandum for chief of staff, handwritten note, 28 July 1943, Administrative Correspondence – Lt Gen Millard Harmon, Jul – Oct 1943, General Historical & Operational Reports, 98-USF 2.1.11, Record Group 338, National Archives, College Park, MD.
[319] Harmon, memorandum, 28 July 1943.
[320] Harmon, memorandum, 28 July 1943.
[321] Louis Morton, *Strategy and Command*, 511.
[322] Louis Morton, *Strategy and Command*, 511.
[323] Harmon, *Army in the South Pacific*, 8.

Figure 19: Harmon on New Georgia. Twining in passenger seat with Griswold, Breene and Strother. Source: Louis Morton, United States Army in World War II, The War in the Pacific, Strategy and Command: The First Two Years (1962; new imprint, Washington, DC: Center of Military History, 2000), 513.

Reconnaissance of the many outlying islands revealed Vella Lavella remained a potential pitfall to Allied operations. The larger Kolombangara Island, whose predominant feature is a massive, extinct volcano, was unsuitable for large-scale airfield operations and subsequently bypassed by South Pacific forces.[324] Instead, soldiers, sailors, and Marines, augmented by New Zealand forces, captured Vella Lavella, effectively surrounding the Japanese forces on Kolombangara with US forces on Vella Lavella to the north and New Georgia to the south. Japanese commanders recognized their predicament and attempted a night evacuation that Allied naval

[324] Harmon, *Army in the South Pacific*, 8.

surface forces intercepted. The ensuing operations crushed the fleeing Japanese forces with minimal losses on the part of the Allies.[325]

Harmon believed that the "results of the New Georgia Campaign almost exceeded expectations."[326] The Americans rebuilt Munda field quickly, and Allied flight operations against Rabaul and the nearby ancillary islands commenced. Land combat operations continued well into the fall of 1943, with elements of the South Pacific forces engaged in clearing operations on Banga Island and Vella Lavella. Soldiers of the 43rd, 37th, and 25th Divisions remained in the field for many more weeks. The duration of these combat operations and harsh conditions took a heavy toll, forcing readiness in many units below sixty percent.[327] This problem complicated matters in just a few weeks.

Bougainville

In the fall of 1943, the pace of operations in the South Pacific had intensified. Allied forces and supplies began a steady flow into the region as the American war machine produced incredible results. With a solid base of operations in Guadalcanal and New Georgia, Halsey and Harmon's focus turned toward Bougainville Island. Bougainville remained the last large island in the Solomon chain, comparable to Guadalcanal in both size and geography. With the ultimate objective of Rabaul in mind, Harmon and Halsey knew Bougainville was required for the establishment of critical airfields.

---

[325] On 2 August 1943, during combat operations near Kolombangara Island, a Japanese warship sank the famous motor torpedo boat PT-109. Based out of Rendova Island, PT-109 was under the command of Lieutenant (JG) John F. Kennedy.

[326] Harmon, *Army in the South Pacific*, 9.

[327] Harmon, *Army in the South Pacific*, 8.

Figure 20: Harmon flying in the Solomons. Source: Millard F. Harmon Papers, 168.604-43, AFHRA.

During the months leading up to the invasion of Bougainville, military planners grappled with several competing plans for the operation. One thought, held primarily by Admiral Halsey, advocated the complete bypassing of Bougainville in a manner similar to the Kolombangara situation. Another idea was for a full invasion of the southern portion of the island that would run headlong into the major Japanese defensive fortifications, a move that would have been "extremely difficult and excessively costly."[328] In September 1943, Halsey sent Harmon to Port Moresby to meet with MacArthur and Kenney and resolve the issue.[329] After great debate, the final plan called for the 3rd Marines to invade the northwest portion of the island near Empress August Bay and Tokorina Point.

---

[328] Harmon, *Army in the South Pacific*, 9.

[329] Wesley Frank Craven and James Lea Cate, eds., *The Army Air Forces in World War II, vol. 4, The Pacific – Guadalcanal to Saipan, August 1942 to July 1944* (Chicago, IL: University of Chicago Press, 1950), 249.

Shortly after daybreak on November 1, the 3rd Marines, under the command of Major General Vandegrift, stormed ashore at Cape Tokorina.[330] Supported by intense naval gunfire and a blanket of over thirty fighter planes from Allied bases in New Georgia, the Marines met the little opposition they expected.[331] Within four short hours, the Marines had expertly established a beachhead at Cape Tokorina, leaving most of its defenders dead.[332] Almost immediately, work began on the construction of an airfield at Tokorina and two auxiliary fields to the north.

With the resounding success of the initial operations, Admiral Halsey shocked Harmon by requesting the removal of the 3rd Marines after only two days of fighting. Halsey intended to rest the 3rd Marines before sending them back into action on short notice against other objectives. Immediately upon hearing the request, Harmon flew to Guadalcanal to confer with Halsey on the subject.[333] Harmon disagreed with Halsey and argued that the move to replace the 3rd Marines with 25th Infantry violated several principles of military operations. In particular, Harmon felt the unnecessary reassignment would jeopardize both units by exposing them to Japanese air and naval attacks during the movement. Furthermore, the insertion of the Americal Division earlier than planned would create a substantial void, leaving the entire theater without a "strategic reserve available for prompt

---

[330] John Miller, Jr., *United States Army in World War II, The War in the Pacific, CARTWHEEL: The Reduction of Rabaul* (Washington, DC: Center of Military History, 1959), 246.
[331] Miller, *CARTWHEEL*, 247.
[332] Miller, *CARTWHEEL*, 246.
[333] Harmon, *Army in the South Pacific*, 10.

commitment to exploit a favorable opportunity or as security in the event of unanticipated reverses."[334]

Halsey heard Harmon's sound arguments but continued with his plan. Within a few weeks, the XIV Corps under General Griswold replaced the 1st Marine Amphibious Corps on Bougainville, and shortly thereafter, the Americal Division replaced the 3rd Marines as well.[335] Halsey respected Harmon's concerns for the welfare of the men on Bougainville and the need to maintain sound military planning during the execution of this mission. In light of Harmon's concerns, Halsey appointed him "his informal deputy for supervising operations of the XIV Corps" on Bougainville to ensure those concerns were addressed.[336] For the third time, Halsey selected Harmon for the direction and execution of major ground combat operations in the South Pacific.[337]

Combat Fatigue in the Army Air Forces

Air operations during this period remained steady and intense. Although living conditions for aircrew and their support personnel had improved since the days of the Cactus Air Force on Guadalcanal, fighting in the South Pacific still levied its lethal fee. The rapid pace of operations of South Pacific ground forces meant aircrew and their machines worked around the clock. Normally, pilots flew combat missions for three months, but after six weeks of combat patrols, one mission every other day, mild operational

---

[334] Lieutenant General M.F. Harmon, Jr., Commanding General, United States Army Forces in the South Pacific Area, to Vice Admiral William F. Halsey, Commander, South Pacific Area, letter, 5 November 1943, Early Records Collection, Operational Archives Branch, Naval Historical Center, Washington, DC.

[335] Miller, *CARTWHEEL*, 266.

[336] Miller, *CARTWHEEL*, 266 – 267.

[337] Harmon, *Army in the South Pacific*, 10.

fatigue was readily apparent.[338] The nature of air combat in the South Pacific, combined with the sparse living conditions and punishing climate, claimed many casualties in the Army Air Forces. Harmon identified these problems as early as fall 1942, during the opening strokes of combat on Guadalcanal.

In November 1942, Harmon saw his flight crews suffering combat fatigue, in particular, the bombardment units flying daily patrols and the pilots and support personnel on Henderson Field. In an effort to provide some rest for his tired aviators, Harmon sent multiple crews in regular intervals for rest periods to Auckland, New Zealand. The few weeks spent at "Aviatoriums" were just enough to recharge the depleted flyers and mix them back into combat rotations.[339] Harmon thought that crews should only fight for six or seven weeks at a time before getting the necessary rest. Harmon saw the same conditions in the RAF during his mission to England as combat units tired during the height of the 'Blitz.' Whereas RAF personnel could drive to the countryside and escape some of the combat conditions, South Pacific personnel required airlift to vacate the area. Unfortunately, Harmon was unable to rotate crews more frequently due to his limited mobility air forces composed of Douglas C-47s Skytrains.

C-47s were in heavy demand during this entire period for theater airlift, medical evacuation, and troop movements, while ferry sorties for crew rest concerns were a lower priority. Additionally, Harmon considered the C-47s "as inadequate to cover the long haul" between the Solomons and Auckland.[340] Therefore, "on grounds of safety, comfort and efficiency Harmon repeatedly...

---

[338] Craven and Cate, *The Pacific – Guadalcanal to Saipan*, 274.
[339] Craven and Cate, *The Pacific – Guadalcanal to Saipan,* 273.
[340] Craven and Cate, *The Pacific – Guadalcanal to Saipan,* 273.

requested C-87s in which he could send down three crews per trip."[341] General Arnold agreed with Harmon's desires to rest his aircrew. Nevertheless, the limited production of eight C-87s per month and competing supply interests around the globe meant Arnold was unable to fill Harmon's request.[342] Intense air operations in support of forces ashore on New Georgia stretched Harmon's men, and with the inadequate resources provided, he could only accomplish a bare minimum amount of rotations.

Relief arrived a few months later during the beginning of the New Georgia operations when a single C-87 arrived for Harmon's use. This one aircraft arrived almost too late because, by this time, medical personnel were dealing with a "growing number of aeroneurosis among their aircrews."[343] In April 1943, Twining began scheduling Auckland runs for exhausted flyers, and after a short while, more aircraft became available.[344] In November, Twining and Harmon were able to arrange regular missions at reasonable intervals, ensuring their combat aviators received approximately nine days of rest in New Zealand between combat tours. Medical personnel in the South Pacific considered Harmon and Twining's efforts as "indispensable."[345]

Unfortunately, again due to limited resources, this much-needed benefit was only available for combat aircrew. Other Army Air Forces personnel working endless hours on airfield construction, aircraft maintenance, or other critical tasks were unable to get the adequate rest they needed.[346] In a survey of

---

[341] Craven and Cate, *The Pacific – Guadalcanal to Saipan,* 273.
[342] Craven and Cate, *The Pacific – Guadalcanal to Saipan,* 274.
[343] Craven and Cate, *The Pacific – Guadalcanal to Saipan,* 274.
[344] Craven and Cate, *The Pacific – Guadalcanal to Saipan,* 274.
[345] Craven and Cate, *The Pacific – Guadalcanal to Saipan,* 275.
[346] Craven and Cate, *The Pacific – Guadalcanal to Saipan,* 275.

Thirteenth Air Force personnel at the end of 1943, the government found nearly 24,232 man-days were lost due to the conditions of life in the South Pacific.[347] Only 219 days were lost due to enemy action.[348] Morale and efficiency of Army Air Forces personnel sank for those unable to benefit from the Auckland rest program. By June, Harmon again outlined this grave problem to Arnold in Washington, DC. Once more, constrained resources and competing interests won out, forcing Harmon to make due with the limited options he possessed.

Figure 21: Harmon in the Solomons. Source: Millard F. Harmon, Jr. Papers, 168.604-43, AFHRA.

[347] Craven and Cate, *The Pacific – Guadalcanal to Saipan,* 275.
[348] Craven and Cate, *The Pacific – Guadalcanal to Saipan,* 275.

Arnold Reassigns Twining

The stress of combat life took its toll on the leaders in the South Pacific as well. In November 1943, Harmon sent Twining, Strother, and Everest on leave for a brief period in the United States. With operations at Bougainville secure, Harmon told the three key members of his air component to enjoy their time off and rejoin with him on the way to the Philippines.[349] The men departed the South Pacific, and upon arrival in California, they received a phone call from Hap Arnold requesting their attendance in Washington, DC. The three South Pacific air leaders boarded their airplane and made the cross-country journey, arriving in Washington around Christmas.[350]

Arnold met them in his office and asked how were "things going down in that awful place?"[351] Twining replied operations were going well and the pace was "picking up a little bit."[352] Expecting more light conversation followed by a month of well-earned leave, Arnold caught Twining off guard with his next comments. "Well, get ready to go, you are leaving tomorrow for Europe," he said. There, Twining was to command the Fifteenth Strategic Air Force operating in Italy. Arnold had reassigned Twining without coordinating with his commander, Miff Harmon.[353] He also removed Strother and Everest from Harmon's organization and

---

[349] General Dean C. Strother, interview by Dr. Murray Green, 2 September 1971, transcript, Box 9, Addendum 10, The Murray Green Collection, US Air Force Academy Library, Colorado Springs, CO.
[350] General Nathan F. Twining, interview by Dr. Murray Green, 2 January 1970, transcript, Box 9, Addendum 20, The Murray Green Collection, US Air Force Academy Library, Colorado Springs, CO.
[351] Twining, interview, 2 January 1970.
[352] Twining, interview, 2 January 1970.
[353] H. H. Arnold, *Global Mission* (New York: Harper & Brothers Publishers, 1949), 502.

reassigned them to other commands around the world.[354] Arnold removed Harmon's most capable airmen; leaders who were with him from the very beginning on Guadalcanal. These men allowed Harmon to concentrate on ground combat concerns while they solved air issues. In a period when Harmon and Arnold exchanged frequent and detailed communiqués outlining daily tactical events, the successful team of Harmon and Twining, a strategic marriage of land and airpower, was severed without even a telegram. Rationale for Arnold's decision is unclear; however, these three men did represent some of the best and brightest the Army Air Forces had to offer. With a developing air war in the Mediterranean, Arnold needed seasoned leaders quickly, and robbing them from the South Pacific was a ready option. It is doubtful that Arnold made this decision to impede Harmon's efforts; however, the manner in which Arnold acted was less than optimum.

"Savage, Suicidal and Somewhat Stupid"[355]

In January 1944, upon assuming command of the ground forces for Bougainville, Harmon found great demands for the maximum utilization of his workforce. Airfield construction and defensive preparations required every available soldier and aviator to give their utmost. Casualties and sicknesses continued to claim many losses while combat stress disorders and neuroses became more prevalent. As unit readiness began to sink, Harmon surveyed his forces and noted a disturbing trend. Harmon understood the

---

[354] Twining, interview, 2 January 1970

[355] Vice Admiral W.F. Halsey, *South Pacific Campaign – Narrative Account*, 3 September 1944, Early Records Collection, Operational Archives Branch, Naval Historical Center, Washington, DC, 11. (Hereafter cited as "Halsey, *South Pacific Campaign*"). Halsey's comment regarding the nature of Japanese tactics and the overall counter attack.

stresses of combat and the need to manage effectively one's forces, but in late January, he found many subordinate commanders were failing in this task.

Harmon wrote all his commanding officers with his concerns. "The present manpower situation has resulted in a shortage of several hundred thousand men in the overall planned strength for the Army," he wrote.[356] This existing shortage had been "aggravated by a tendency of some commanders to recommend discharge of men who could render further useful service if properly assigned and trained." Harmon outlined many physically qualified men were serving in positions that could be filled by other, lesser-qualified personnel. Harkening back to his days at West Point, he also scolded commanders for failing to make adequate provisions for troop hygiene, sanitation, and disease prevention. These deficiencies resulted in the preventable loss of many well-qualified men. Harmon ordered his officers to make the necessary changes immediately "to ensure that the conservation of manpower is practiced" in their respective commands.[357]

Meanwhile, allied air and naval operations repeatedly pounded Japanese positions along the southern coast of Bougainville from November 1943 until early spring 1944. By March, the remaining enemy forces on Bougainville had lost all air and sea protection. Japanese commanders recognized their perilous situation. Severed from reinforcements and marooned on Bougainville, the Japanese

---

[356] Lieutenant General M.F. Harmon, Commanding General, United States Army Forces in the South Pacific Area, to USAFISPA subordinate commanders, 24 January 1944, Administrative Correspondence, General Historical & Operational Reports, 98-USF 2-1.11, Record Group 338, National Archives, College Park, MD. (Hereafter cited as "Harmon, Maximum Utilization of Manpower Memorandum").

[357] Harmon, Maximum Utilization of Manpower Memorandum.

had few options remaining. During this time, Japanese commanders mistakenly assumed that the main Allied advance was in southern Bougainville, the area of intense air and sea attacks, not Tokorina. They eventually realized this mistake, but it was too late. In response to the tardy detection of the main Allied effort near Empress Augusta Bay, Japanese commanders put to work plans for a substantial counterattack in March, which Harmon and his other commanders uncovered in advance. XIV Corps soldiers completed preparations and defensive positions before the Japanese assault began on March 8.

The attack was led by the Japanese Sixth Army Division and "came against positions that had been carefully prepared in-depth, with well-prepared fields of fire and manned by well-disciplined, healthy and ready-to-go troops of the 37th and Americal Divisions."[358] Possessing strong defenses and the benefit of interior lines, General Griswold was able to repulse all of the Japanese advances.[359] Japanese artillery attacks on the allied positions did cause damage, but not enough to prevent decisive air operations from the three airfields at Tokorina Point. Admiral Halsey wrote to his superiors that the Japanese soldiers were "mowed down without mercy."[360] Harmon also recorded the successful defensive efforts. By "the end of March, the Jap effort had completely expended itself," Harmon wrote.[361] Both Halsey and Harmon estimated that American forces killed over 10,000 enemy soldiers

---

[358] Halsey, *South Pacific Campaign*, 11.
[359] Miller, *CARTWHEEL*, 355.
[360] Halsey, *South Pacific Campaign*, 12.
[361] Harmon, *Army in the South Pacific*, 10.

of an original force numbering approximately 12,000, at a total cost of 263 members of the XIV Corps.[362]

Other operations around the area were ongoing throughout March. MacArthur's forces captured positions in the Admiralties and along the north coast of New Guinea and the western portion of New Britain.[363] With the fall of Bougainville later that month and with the creation of new airfields throughout the theater, the remaining Japanese strongholds at Rabaul and Kavieng laid open for air and sea attacks. On March 20, South Pacific forces took six days to capture Emirau, a small island north of New Ireland. Within six weeks, engineers completed the construction of a new airfield there that eventually garrisoned over 18,000 men.[364]

Harmon's Thoughts on SOPAC

As operations on Bougainville and Emirau subsided, Harmon solicited inputs from his senior commanders for his after-action report. By early 1944, Harmon had witnessed firsthand all of the major combat operations in the South Pacific. He personally participated in troop landings, visited and fought with forces ashore, and even flew reconnaissance missions, winning a Distinguished Flying Cross for one such sortie.[365] His lessons, therefore, came after great thought, rich with valuable experience and eyewitness knowledge. A commander not afraid to see the battle conditions firsthand continued to win admiration of his troops and superiors.

---

[362] Harmon, *Army in the South Pacific*, 10, Halsey, *South Pacific Campaign*, 12, and Miller, *CARTWHEEL*, 378.
[363] Miller, *CARTWHEEL*, 379.
[364] Miller, *CARTWHEEL*, 380.
[365] Millard F. Harmon, III (Son of Miff Harmon), interviewed by the author, 23 April 2007.

Harmon's main points in his memorandum focused on the need to streamline joint operations. From initial planning efforts until the mission objectives were reached, Harmon wrote that individual service idiosyncrasies reduced overall effectiveness. This was most evident in the different supply and logistical considerations required for joint operations. "Every effort should be made to standardize all types of equipment to be used by every arm or service involved," he wrote.[366] Because of similar missions between Marine and Army units but different operating procedures and equipment, "parallel supply systems [compete] for critical shipping space to the forward areas."[367] Additionally, situations arose "where one service [had] a surplus while another [had] a severe shortage of spare parts for comparable equipment."[368] Harmon also felt that this meant that the "exchange of equipment between services" during relief operations was impossible.[369]

Harmon also made tactical observations about his tenure in SOPAC. First, he advocated an appreciation for local cultures and languages was necessary to operate in foreign lands. "Personnel, experienced in handling natives, [are] essential," he stated.[370] Harmon understood the nature of expeditionary warfare and the reliance on local labor and indigenous support for intelligence-gathering purposes.

---

[366] Lieutenant General M.F. Harmon, Commanding General, United States Army Forces in the South Pacific Area, *Lessons Learned from Joint Operations in the New Georgia and Bougainville Operations*, 5 February 1944, General Historical & Operational Reports, 98-USF2-0.4, Record Group 338, National Archives, College Park, MD. (Hereafter cited as "Harmon, *Lessons Learned*").
[367] Harmon, *Lessons Learned*.
[368] Harmon, *Lessons Learned*.
[369] Harmon, *Lessons Learned*.
[370] Harmon, *Lessons Learned*.

Second, he warned that jungle operations and low-precision aerial bombardment were incompatible. "Dive bombing rather than high-level bombing must be the rule for ground support," he wrote.[371] Harmon had advocated in-depth mission planning between air and ground forces since his experiences in the Punitive Expedition. In World War II, this meant air forces required close coordination with ground troops to prevent fratricide and unnecessary collateral damage. Harmon also stressed these factors during his Infantry school and ACTS exercises in the late-1930s. His observations reflected a great deal of maturity, emphasizing the critical nature of staff work and logistical planning during all operations. Harmon's continued emphasis on joint interoperability and the need to overcome service individualism for mission accomplishment remain valid today.

A New Job

The fall of Emirau in the spring of 1944 marked the end of offensive operations for the South Pacific forces.[372] In the previous twenty months, since July 1942, on Guadalcanal, South Pacific forces, several times under the command of Millard F. Harmon, destroyed major portions of the Japanese air, sea, and land forces. In a letter from the commander of the XIV Corps, General Griswold credited Harmon with many of the South Pacific successes. "The XIV Corps has been glad to present you with two victorious operations," he wrote.[373] The soldiers of the XIV Corps and other

---

[371] Harmon, *Lessons Learned.*

[372] Harmon, *Army in the South Pacific*, 10 and Halsey, *South Pacific Campaign*, 10.

[373] Major General O.W. Griswold, Commanding General, XIV Corps, to Lieutenant General M.F. Harmon, Commanding General, United States Army Forces in the South Pacific Area, letter, 25 April 1944, Administrative Correspondence, General Historical & Operational Reports, 98-USF 2-1.11,

Allied units captured numerous airfields, destroyed hundreds of airplanes, killed thousands of soldiers, and bypassed another 100,000 soldiers on the way to reducing the main Japanese stronghold at Rabaul and Kavieng.[374] The gloomy days on Guadalcanal, when the fate of the American effort was uncertain, gave way to much faster operations in the Russells, New Georgia, and Bougainville.

Similarly, forces in the Central Pacific under the command of Admiral Nimitz enjoyed many successes and pushed the Japanese back nearly 2,400 miles from Pearl Harbor. By the summer of 1944, the Americans, "poised on the westernmost of the Marshalls," reversed all previous Japanese offensives and stood ready to attack the home islands.[375] This meant the formation, organization, and administration of a massive Central Pacific air force. Equipped with the new Boeing B-29 Superfortress, Nimitz' forces would be able to strike at the heart of Japan in a few months. This new challenge required enormous logistical planning and a consolidated headquarters to manage the influx of new aircraft and personnel. It also required leadership trained in the methods of Pacific warfare with a keen eye for the development of strategic airfields to strike Tokyo. With the conclusion of offensive combat operations in the South Pacific, Admiral Nimitz made the logical choice and hired the most tested Army Air Forces general in the Pacific.

Record Group 338, National Archives, College Park, MD. Griswold further wrote, "We are still counting ourselves as your boys until we get thrown out."

[374] Miller, *CARTWHEEL*, 381.

[375] Craven and Cate, *The Pacific – Guadalcanal to Saipan*, 671.

Chapter Nine: Navigating Treacherous Waters

> "If you find it beyond your capacity to reconcile these conflicting loyalties, then I shall expect you to acquaint me with that fact; and if I find that my interests are not being adequately cared for, I shall not hesitate to resolve this difficulty by relieving you of further responsibility as my deputy."
>
> *H.H. Arnold to M.F. Harmon, June 6, 1944*

> "Harmon told me...[maintain your] integrity in the political atmosphere, which is getting tougher and tougher in Washington, if you don't why you're going to lose it. It's all going to be political..."
>
> *General Dean C. Strother, April 1976*

Strategic air attacks against Japanese targets had been ongoing for some time by the spring of 1944. As part of Operation MATTERHORN, B-29s based in China struck cities in Japan as early as 1943. The Joint Chiefs of Staff, pressed by Hap Arnold, soon recognized the need for an entirely new command to oversee B-29 strikes from recently captured Pacific island bases. "Established under command principles radically different from those governing the other Army air forces," officials created the Twentieth Air Force on April 4, 1944, and directed that its commander report to authorities in Washington, DC, regarding the use of strategic airpower against Japan, not to theater commanders.[376] The existence of such a command, operating administratively and logistically within a senior military commander's theater yet reporting for operational matters to another outside of that theater, made for frequent and difficult clashes between military heavyweights.

According to the Joint Chiefs of Staff, the Twentieth Air Force "operated directly under the JCS with the Commanding General, AAF as executive agent."[377] Theater commanders provided suitable bases for Twentieth Air Force operations and handled all logistical obligations while operational direction resided outside of their purview. Arnold himself maintained "direct communication with [Very Long Range] leaders in the field, advising appropriate theater commanders."[378] This arrangement meant Arnold determined the Twentieth Air Force's scheme of operations in Washington, DC, thousands of miles away from the pilots and planes of the Twentieth Air Force.

Initially, command issues for the Twentieth Air Force operated efficiently, with Arnold and the JCS providing direction and Brigadier General Haywood 'Possum' Hansell, Jr., who was the Twentieth Air Force Chief of Staff, executing orders. However, by spring 1944, after Nimitz' forces captured the Marianas, it became apparent that Twentieth Air Force operations were changing. After

---

[376] Wesley Frank Craven and James Lea Cate, eds., *The Army Air Forces in World War II, vol. 5, The Pacific – Matterhorn to Nagasaki, June 1944 to August 1945* (Chicago, IL: University of Chicago Press, 1953), 33.
[377] Craven and Cate, *The Pacific – Matterhorn to Nagasaki*, 38. (The Army Air Forces used VLR (Very Long Range) and VHB (Very Heavy Bombers) interchangeably and indiscriminately when discussing B-29 matters.)
[378] Craven and Cate, *The Pacific – Matterhorn to Nagasaki*, 38.

the seizure of the Marianas, which rendered the Chinese bases less valuable, the XX Bomber Command moved its operations to the Central Pacific Theater, thereby increasing the amount of assets available in the Twentieth Air Force. Aware that this move would thrust major Army Air Forces operations into the Navy's theater, Arnold recalled Millard Harmon to Washington, DC, to discuss the matter.

In June 1944, Harmon and his staff traveled to Washington, DC, under secret orders to discuss the strategic bombardment of Japan and the future of air power in the Pacific. From the very beginning, Arnold felt the Pacific Theater and its lack of proper command arrangements complicated the conduct of effective air warfare. Arnold's 1942 visit on board the USS *Argonne* had convinced him that no unity of command existed in the Pacific Theater.[379] The Navy preferred the task force concept and parceling small units of airpower to each task force. As Arnold introduced the new B-29s in theater, he was risking Navy interference in the strategic air effort against Japan. To prevent this from happening and to maintain a degree of overall control, Arnold retained power over Pacific B-29 operations in his headquarters in Washington, DC.[380]

Controlling bomber operations against Japan from Washington was difficult. The separation of the main headquarters from its operations resulted in communication problems and material delays.[381] Arnold, therefore, needed a capable deputy in theater to represent his intentions. This individual had to be well-versed in air combat planning and organization but even more skilled at

[379] Craven and Cate, *The Pacific – Matterhorn to Nagasaki*, 35.
[380] H. H. Arnold, *Global Mission* (New York: Harper & Brothers Publishers, 1949), 348.
[381] Craven and Cate, *The Pacific – Matterhorn to Nagasaki*, 93.

negotiating the difficult command structures in the Pacific. In a theater where relationships and personalities mattered, Arnold made the natural decision to select a leader who had demonstrated these qualities for the previous two years. Harmon's success in the South Pacific and close ties with senior Navy leaders in theater made him the logical choice.

Even though Harmon was the preferred deputy for Arnold in theater, Hap harbored reservations regarding Harmon's ability to balance the needs of the Twentieth Air Force without yielding to the desires of Admiral Nimitz. As early as April 16, Nimitz had proposed the creation of a separate organization to lead Army Air Forces operations, excluding B-29s, in the Central Pacific with Harmon at the helm.[382] This relationship could empower Harmon to wage, single-handedly, a Navy-led air war using both Navy and Army assets against Japan with minimal Army Air Forces input from outside of the Pacific Theater. Concerned with the possible conflicting interests, Arnold discussed with Harmon the prospects of his new assignment as deputy commander and how those related to his pending appointment as Nimitz' air boss. "Arnold underscored Harmon's dual role that would put him 'in a most difficult position,'" balancing the needs of Arnold, as commander of the Twentieth Air Force, and Nimitz, as Commander in Chief of Pacific Oceans Area (CINCPOA).[383] Arnold emphasized his displeasure with the Navy Task Force system. He illustrated to Harmon that his organization would be significantly different from the command structure of other Army Air Forces units.[384] Arnold

---

[382] Craven and Cate, *The Pacific – Matterhorn to Nagasaki*, 510.
[383] Dr. Murray Green, "General Harmon's Split Command" (working note cards, box 52, 8.60, The Murray Green Collection, US Air Force Academy Library, Colorado Springs, CO). (Hereafter cited as "Green, Harmon's Split Command").
[384] Green, Harmon's Split Command.

hoped this command situation would be temporary, and during such time, Harmon could advise Nimitz on the proper "employment of land-based forces."[385] Arnold also wanted him to stress to Nimitz the eventual need for a vertical command structure and the establishment of a single air command in the Pacific.

Battling 'Big Army'

Harmon's new job presented another unique problem. As AAFPOA, under Nimitz, and deputy commander of the Twentieth Air Force, working for Arnold, Harmon no longer served as the senior Army officer in theater. Lieutenant General Robert Richardson, then serving as the Commanding General US Army Forces in the Central Pacific Area (USAFICPA), held that position.[386] With the creation of AAFPOA, the War Department envisaged the subsequent creation of the United States Army Forces POA (USAFPOA), possibly led by Richardson. Initial plans for the creation of AAFPOA had Harmon reporting to Richardson and then to Nimitz, inserting an additional layer of non-Air Force bureaucracy in the chain of command. Harmon heard of this proposal and immediately offered a counterproposal that put himself directly under Nimitz and on "an equal status with USAFPOA except for ultimate court-martial jurisdiction."[387] With Harmon's counterproposal, Arnold went to the War Department and asked to put Harmon on "par with General Richardson."[388] When the War Department levied their final policy, Harmon and Arnold "won major concessions."[389] Although Arnold and Harmon failed to

---

[385] Green, Harmon's Split Command.
[386] Craven and Cate, *The Pacific – Matterhorn to Nagasaki*, 507.
[387] Craven and Cate, *The Pacific – Matterhorn to Nagasaki*, 511.
[388] Green, Harmon's Split Command.
[389] Craven and Cate, *The Pacific – Matterhorn to Nagasaki*, 511.

secure total independence for AAFPOA, the War Department eventually allowed Harmon to report to Nimitz directly on operational issues.[390] This was a major concession, but it caused great friction between Harmon and Richardson.

Highlighting the tension between Harmon's role as AAFPOA and as the Deputy Commander of the Twentieth Air Force, Arnold told his friend of thirty years they needed to maintain open and frank lines of communication regarding Harmon's new assignment. Arnold presented his own concerns "very bluntly and very frankly" because he felt it "very necessary that [Harmon] have a clear understanding" of his future position.[391] If Harmon could not synchronize his competing obligations, Arnold expected him to absolve himself of the command arrangements and ask for a replacement. Harmon, acknowledging Arnold's concerns and understanding the gravity of the situation, returned to the Pacific Theater for this incredible challenge. With Harmon's acceptance, Arnold believed he had secured the "strong hand" in the Pacific he needed to handle the swirling eddies of inter-service rivalries.[392]

On July 10, the War Department finalized these command relationships. An Operations Plans Division memorandum, signed by General Marshall, established USAFPOA and appointed General Richardson as the first commander. General Richardson was also responsible for command of the Hawaiian Department, and in both roles, he reported directly to CINCPOA, Admiral Nimitz. Concurrently, the War Department created AAFPOA and appointed Harmon its first commander. Similar to Richardson, Harmon reported directly to Nimitz for "all matters pertaining to the

---

[390] Craven and Cate, *The Pacific – Matterhorn to Nagasaki*, 511.
[391] Green, Harmon's Split Command.
[392] Craven and Cate, *The Pacific – Matterhorn to Nagasaki*, 510.

preparation of plans, operation, training, and disposition of his forces."[393]

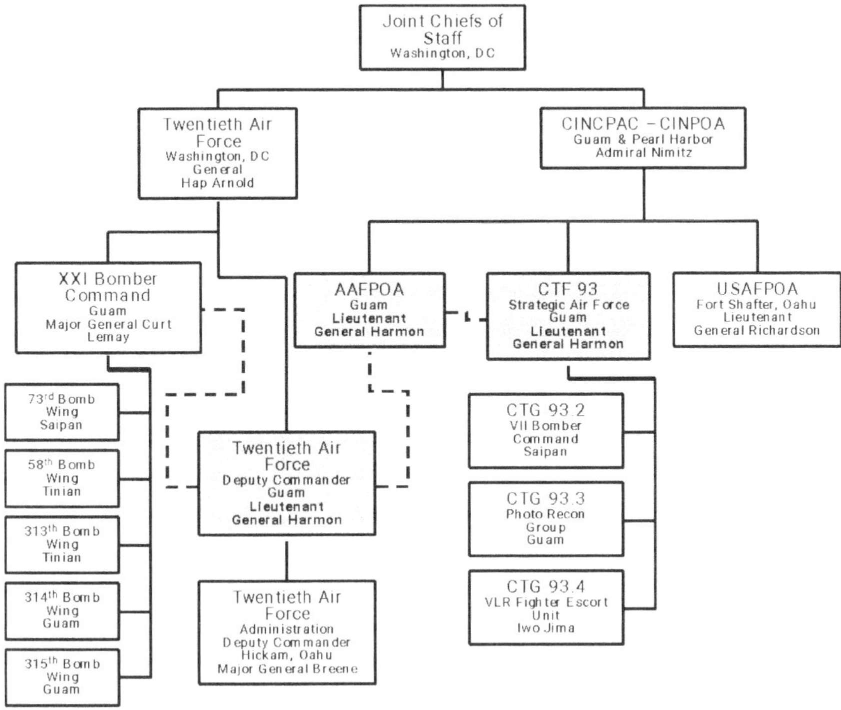

Figure 22: Command Relationships in 1944. Source: Wesley Frank Craven and James Lea Cate, eds., The Army Air Forces in World War II, vol. 5, The Pacific – Matterhorn to Nagasaki, June 1944 to August 1945 (Chicago, IL: University of Chicago Press, 1953), 527. Modified by the author.

Putting Theory into Practice

Six weeks after returning to the Pacific, Harmon realized that the command relationships of the Twentieth Air Force, convoluted

[393] General G.C. Marshall, Chief of Staff, War Department, to Commanding General, United States Army Forces, Central Pacific Area and Commanding General, United States Army Forces, South Pacific Area, letter, 10 July 1944, 702.201, IRIS No.00250158, AFHRA.

from the beginning, were even more confusing than originally intended and required further clarification. Writing to Arnold, Harmon requested an illumination of his authority as the Deputy Commander of the Twentieth Air Force. His responsibilities, in "dual capacity as COMGEN AAFPOA and as Deputy Commander of the Twentieth Air Force, are involved and difficult at best," Harmon wrote, and "any lack of clarity...[adds] to the confusion."[394] After more inquiries by Harmon, Arnold responded on September 25. Arnold wrote that he fully intended to delegate many of the Twentieth Air Force command responsibilities to Harmon specifically because of his proximity to the area of operations. Those tasks, however, consisted only of minor staff activities such as "promotions and awards."[395] Arnold alone retained oversight for critical functions such as "support of Pacific forces" and "direct operational control" of the combat aircraft.[396] "You will, of course, be fully advised in order that you may discharge the responsibilities of Deputy Commander as assigned by General Marshall's directive of 10 July 1944."[397]

Harmon's attempt to gain clarity from Arnold was unproductive. In what initially appeared as an opportunity for more control over theater air forces as the Deputy Commander for the Twentieth Air Force, Harmon now seemed to have fewer prerogatives. Harmon requested urgent action for the resolution of these issues and received none. Lieutenant General Barney Giles,

---

[394] Lieutenant General M.F. Harmon, Commanding General, Army Air Forces Pacific Oceans Area, to General H.H. Arnold, Commanding General, Army Air Forces, letter, 15 August 1944, MICFILM 28195, IRIS No. 002053381, AFHRA.
[395] General H.H. Arnold, Commanding General, Army Air Forces, to Lieutenant General M.F. Harmon, Commanding General, Army Air Forces Pacific Oceans Area, letter, 25 September 1944, MICFILM 28195, IRIS No. 002053381, AFHRA.
[396] Arnold to Harmon, 25 September 1944.
[397] Arnold to Harmon, 25 September 1944.

serving as Chief of Staff to Arnold, wrote Harmon about the slow pace at which the War Department moved to resolve command issues in the Pacific. "As you, no doubt recall," Giles stated, "change in some rather fundamental and long-established policies are involved, which makes speedy action rather difficult to obtain."[398] Harmon's difficult command situation only worsened over time. With the introduction of the XXI Bomber Command, the treacherous waters of organizational responsibilities reached a boiling point.

Building the Foundation

As the Commanding General of AAFPOA, Harmon went to work building the massive infrastructure required for Very Heavy Bomber (VHB) operations in the Pacific. Almost immediately, though, he ran into familiar shipping and logistical challenges. As the senior representative to Nimitz for Army Air Forces issues, Harmon consistently lobbied for elevated delivery and engineering priorities regarding VHB operations. "Harmon devoted his energies unstintingly to expediting the construction of bases and the establishment of VHB units in theater."[399] In the meantime, Nimitz, though sympathetic to the VHB program, balanced the competing demands for highly sought shipping spaces, sometimes at the expense of Harmon's needs. By August 1944, in spite of these constraints, construction efforts were proceeding at several B-29 sites.

Harmon toured and selected nearly every VHB base in the Pacific. Ultimately, his command created VHB bases at Guam,

---

[398] Lieutenant General B.M. Giles, Chief of Staff, Army Air Forces, to Lieutenant General M.F. Harmon, Deputy Commander, Twentieth Air Force, letter, 26 September 1944, 702.161-2, IRIS No. 00249803, AFHRA.
[399] Craven and Cate, *The Pacific – Matterhorn to Nagasaki*, 514 – 515.

Saipan, and Tinian and a massive air depot on Guam. Flight range, available construction materials, and enemy activity all influenced the selection of VHB bases. In many cases, enemy activity remained strong well after the Americans had captured the small islands. During one visit to the Pacific in 1944, Hap Arnold witnessed the intense enemy activity firsthand. "The Japanese were still being killed, still being brought in, walking and surrendering" many months after the Americans captured one island, he remembered.[400] As the Army Air Force's official history relayed, "determined enemy resistance in the Marianas upset" all construction schedules.[401]

Navy priorities also took their toll on building efforts at VHB locations. Admiral Nimitz' proclamation regarding the establishment of CINCPOA forward headquarters on Guam and the subsequent staging of all ground forces there for ensuing efforts against Formosa complicated Harmon's efforts. Harmon wrote to Washington, DC, that the decision would delay VHB progress by at least 100 days.[402] This delay sent ripples through many of the Air Staff's ongoing deployment actions as new units and personnel pooled on the west coast of the United States awaiting completion of the Guam VHB installations.

In response to the wrinkle, Harmon devised a new plan to compensate for the loss of additional infrastructure on Guam. After surveying the other VHB sites, Harmon concluded that Tinian could support a larger VHB presence. On August 17, Harmon proposed to Nimitz "a major revision of VHB plans which promised to save the

---

[400] Arnold, *Global Mission*, 563.
[401] Craven and Cate, *The Pacific – Matterhorn to Nagasaki*, 515.
[402] Craven and Cate, *The Pacific – Matterhorn to Nagasaki*, 515.

situation."[403] Harmon's plan involved a full-scale reprioritization of construction efforts, which in turn required Nimitz' approval for increased shipping priorities and logistical support. Even though completion of Harmon's plans took several more months, his decisive action in August resulted in combat operations commencing in November 1944.[404]

Nimitz and Harmon continued to grapple over VHB construction priorities into 1945. On more than one occasion,

Figure 23: AAFPOA Commander. Lt Gen Harmon in front of a B-29 Superfortress from the cover of the Brief. Source: Cover of Brief magazine, 27 March 1945, Millard F. Harmon, Jr. Papers, 702.952, Air Force Historical Research Agency.

---

[403] Craven and Cate, *The Pacific – Matterhorn to Nagasaki*, 516.
[404] Craven and Cate, *The Pacific – Matterhorn to Nagasaki*, 517.

Harmon traveled hundreds of miles to meet Nimitz for face-to-face discussions. In the meantime, Harmon's engineers and construction teams worked relentlessly to complete the airfields under intense Pacific conditions. Unlike the small dirt or mesh strips required for fighter aircraft, B-29s needed longer, hardened paved surfaces. This meant engineers needed to blast through coral formations and flatten jungles to build a single runway. By December, when bomber units began to arrive in Guam, Harmon's men had built headquarters buildings, mess halls, latrines, washrooms, and support facilities in record time.[405]

By February 1945, Harmon's men completed construction of his own headquarters on Guam. From there, he continued to press Nimitz for the prioritization of construction efforts at the remaining VHB sites. Harmon was incessant on the need to establish airfields first, from which B-29s could strike at the industrial heart of Japan. In many respects, his pestering paid off because he was able to secure "adequate priorities for B-29 building programs that frequently ran counter to Navy demands in a Navy theater."[406]

XXI Bomber Command

It did not take very long for the command relationships in the Pacific to become even more complicated with the introduction of the XXI Bomber Command at Guam. The XXI Bomber Command, subordinate to the Twentieth Air Force, was the successor to the XX Bomber Command that had attacked Japanese strategic targets with B-29s based in the China-Burma-India Theater. With the acquisition of the Marianas sites, the XX Bomber Command efforts

---

[405] Craven and Cate, *The Pacific – Matterhorn to Nagasaki*, 521.
[406] Craven and Cate, *The Pacific – Matterhorn to Nagasaki*, xvii.

from China became less important and were absorbed into the larger Pacific effort.

Brigadier General 'Possum' Hansell, a "veteran of the B-29 program," relinquished his position in the Twentieth Air Force and served as the commander of the XXI Bomber Command effective August 29, 1944.[407] For the next five months, Hansell struggled to produce results in line with Arnold's expectations. High winds and persistent weather frustrated many of Hansell's hundred-plane attacks against the industrial zones of Japan. Repeatedly, Brigadier General Lauris Norstad, Hap Arnold's Twentieth Air Force Chief of Staff in Washington, DC, challenged Hansell to improve results. Additionally, Norstad pushed Hansell to experiment with incendiary raids, a tactic proposed by many to exploit the wooden and paper buildings found in Tokyo. Hansell attempted some incendiary missions but still failed to produce the results Arnold demanded. After a few more weeks of substandard attacks, the Army Air Forces chief dispatched Norstad to the Pacific. On January 20, 1945, Hansell was relieved of command and replaced by Major General Curtis LeMay.[408]

Curt LeMay was Arnold's fix-it man, his go-to operator with a history of righting poor units and quickly producing great results. Arnold installed LeMay and gave him the fullest autonomy possible with the expectation of improved performance. Within a few weeks, the XXI Bomber Command delivered. In retrospect, it is unclear if the XXI Bomber Command improvements were the results of measures instituted by Hansell prior to his departure or

---

[407] Craven and Cate, *The Pacific – Matterhorn to Nagasaki*, 546.
[408] Craven and Cate, *The Pacific – Matterhorn to Nagasaki*, 567.

LeMay's policies. Nonetheless, LeMay received the credit for the quick turnaround.

Harmon and LeMay, unlike Arnold and LeMay, did not enjoy a warm relationship. From the very beginning, the two men clashed over command responsibilities, operational control of aircraft, and missions performed by the B-29s. Harmon, both eighteen years senior to LeMay in age and time in service, found LeMay to be operating outside of the prescribed bounds of his command. On the one hand, Harmon wanted more control over LeMay's operations, including tactics and targets. On the other hand, LeMay firmly believed that he worked directly for Arnold and did not need to coordinate with Harmon.

In January 1945, Harmon and LeMay fought vigorously over the control of Very Long Range (VLR) escort fighters. Harmon maintained that he needed to control VLR fighters as the Deputy Commander of the Twentieth Air Force or at least as the Commanding General of AAFPOA to ensure unity of effort for all Pacific operations. Harmon feared that leaving the VLR fighters solely for the use of the XXI Bomber Command operations would render them "frozen" and unavailable for use during other operations.[409] Similar to his positions in previous scenarios, Harmon was concerned with ensuring "every aircraft [was] used to its full capacity in winning the war."[410]

---

[409] Craven and Cate, *The Pacific – Matterhorn to Nagasaki*, 530.
[410] Craven and Cate, *The Pacific – Matterhorn to Nagasaki*, 530.

Figure 24: Harmon in 1944. Photo is signed "This from Pop for Dearest Helen" (his daughter). Source: Millard F. Harmon, III. Picture in author's collection.

LeMay countered with a strong message to Arnold in Washington, "insisting that he must have absolute operational control of the fighters" for his own B-29s.[411] Arnold agreed with LeMay and "reaffirmed his decision to limit Harmon's operational control" to ancillary operations against Iwo Jima and Okinawa, but not the Japanese mainland.[412] Again, Harmon's attempts to clarify his role as the Deputy Commander of the Twentieth Air Force were frustrated by Arnold. This time, a subordinate commander, eighteen years his junior, who learned to fly while Harmon was the

[411] Craven and Cate, *The Pacific – Matterhorn to Nagasaki*, 530.
[412] Craven and Cate, *The Pacific – Matterhorn to Nagasaki*, 530.

Commandant of the Air Corps Primary Flying School, won the debate.

Colonel Sol Rosenblatt, a member of the Army Air Forces staff in Washington, wrote LeMay in January about LeMay's dealings with Harmon. "I recommend you not be taken in by any bull from anyone. I don't care who he is," he wrote.[413] "The fellows you have [out there in the Pacific] in my honest opinion have been blinded by 'star dust' in their eyes, and politics between the 21st, the Guam depot and AAFPOA have run rampant."[414] Rosenblatt went on to say that "some are too old to cure" and that he preferred to "use the surgeon's scalpel" to remedy the situation.[415]

The strained relations between LeMay and Harmon are also reflected in letters between LeMay and Norstad. LeMay wrote, "General Harmon is due here today, and I have a long list of troubles to present him," though LeMay was "not hopeful of a satisfactory solution."[416] All the while, Harmon continued his requests for further clarification regarding his role as Deputy Commander of the Twentieth Air Force vis-à-vis the XXI Bomber Command. Finally, having reached his limit, Miff Harmon made plans to travel to Washington, DC, to discuss personally the matter with Arnold. Rosenblatt wrote to LeMay upon hearing of Harmon's travel plans and stated, "you probably know that General Harmon is coming in here. We don't know what all he is going to raise, but

---

[413] Colonel S.A. Rosenblatt, Air Corps, to Major General C.E. LeMay, Commanding General, Twentieth Bomber Command, letter, 10 January 1945, in The Papers of Curtis E. LeMay, Library of Congress, Washington, DC.
[414] Rosenblatt to LeMay, 10 January 1945.
[415] Rosenblatt to LeMay, 10 January 1945.
[416] Major General C.E. LeMay, Commanding General, Twentieth Bomber Command, to Brigadier General L. Norstad, Twentieth Air Force, letter, 31 January 1945, in The Papers of Curtis E. LeMay, Library of Congress, Washington, DC.

General Norstad is fully prepared."[417] Harmon summoned his chief of staff, Brigadier General James Anderson, and the executive to the deputy commander for operations, Colonel William Ball, to join him on the journey to Washington, DC. The three men and a crew of aviators departed Kwajalein in Harmon's temporary transport shortly after sunset on February 26, 1945. The flight never made it out of the Pacific.

The Importance of 'Box-ology'[418]

Harmon's quest for command clarification may appear to be a power grab. However, the delineation of command roles is a significant issue. Command interactions define one's area of accountability. They outline avenues of resources, relationships to other subordinate and superior agencies, and they determine where the weight of effort will fall during a crisis. Furthermore, particularly in combat, organizational schemas determine which commanders have the ultimate authority and responsibility to send men into battle. Harmon had served the last two and half years battling the Japanese and the organizational nightmare that was the Pacific Theater.

"General Harmon had one of the most difficult and complex assignments of the war," according to the official history of the Army Air Forces in World War II.[419] Even while in the South Pacific Theater, and especially afterward, Harmon built the organizational

---

[417] Colonel S.A. Rosenblatt, Air Corps, to Major General C.E. LeMay, Commanding General, Twentieth Bomber Command, letter, 23 February 1945, in The Papers of Curtis E. LeMay, Library of Congress, Washington, DC. This letter and previous letters between Rosenblatt and LeMay are very informal. Colonel Rosenblatt often refers to LeMay as 'Curt,' implying a previous working relationship.

[418] Getting the organizational boxes correct.

[419] Craven and Cate, *The Pacific – Matterhorn to Nagasaki*, 525.

structure necessary to wage an air war directly against Japan. He also oversaw the massive construction efforts of many of the VHB installations. During this entire time, Harmon wore at least three 'hats of responsibility.' First, Harmon reported directly to Arnold as the Deputy Commander of the Twentieth Air Force, the independent striking arm of the Army Air Forces against Japan. Second, he served Admiral Nimitz as the senior Army Air Forces commander for all air operations. Under the title of Commanding General AAFPOA, Harmon retained control of all air forces outside of the Twentieth Air Force yet worked to synchronize the efforts between the two.

Finally, Nimitz appointed Harmon the commander of Strategic Air Force POA (Task Force 93) in December 1944. Command of Strategic Air Force POA gave Harmon operational control of "all Army and Navy land-based bombers and fighters" in Nimitz' theater.[420] Moreover, Harmon controlled Marine aviation squadrons as well as Seventh Air Force units.[421] This represented the third group of air force assets, organizations, bases, logistical efforts, and personnel that Harmon oversaw. Each of these air groups had different objectives and different chains of command, many times conflicting with one another. These "difficult and irritating jurisdictional problems" led to Harmon's "unique and always indefinite status" in the Pacific.[422] Harmon was never able to gain the clarity he sought.

Harmon's quest for operational control of B-29 actions against Japan is understandable. As the commander of AAFPOA and Strategic Air Force POA, Harmon was in the perfect position to

---

[420] Craven and Cate, *The Pacific – Matterhorn to Nagasaki*, 529.
[421] Craven and Cate, *The Pacific – Matterhorn to Nagasaki*, xvii.
[422] Craven and Cate, *The Pacific – Matterhorn to Nagasaki*, 525.

synchronize and sequence all of the major air operations in the theater. Additionally, Harmon knew that command of air operations from Washington, DC was difficult to effectuate. Reminiscent of his disdain for geographically removed headquarters during the RAF operations in 1941, Harmon knew his forward location was more appropriate, giving him the up-close insight necessary to command this unique organization. He also understood the nature of the enemy, difficulty of weather conditions, and the importance of suitable fields. For these reasons, he was inclined to interpret the duty of Deputy Commander of the Twentieth Air Force as one who had "virtual control of all B-29 operations."[423] Arnold, LeMay, and their staffs, however, refused to accept Harmon's position. For Arnold and other Army Air Forces airmen, Harmon's position as AAFPOA "literally disqualified him for operational control because it would jeopardize the Twentieth Air Force's position in relation to the Navy."[424]

Arnold's fear of Navy intrusion had led to the consolidation of authority in Washington, DC. Arnold understood the nature of the command organization in the Pacific Theater, and rightly expected the Navy would tear apart Army Air Forces units, thereby minimizing the impact of large bomber operations. With industrial Germany in rubble, Arnold focused his attention on the destruction of Japan with the B-29 Superfortress. In his mind, subjugating those platforms to the Navy would relegate them to tactical missions at best and leave the heart of Japan safe.

---

[423] Craven and Cate, *The Pacific – Matterhorn to Nagasaki*, xvii.
[424] Craven and Cate, *The Pacific – Matterhorn to Nagasaki*, 531.

Chapter Ten: Finishing Where He Started

> "Here we are down there in Guadalcanal, fighting a losing war. We were losing the war, and the Air Force was getting no equipment whatsoever. Miff Harmon was the boss of the air and he was highly respected by the Navy, and Arnold wouldn't give him a damn thing. He wouldn't give him a decent airplane to fly in. That's how he got killed, flying a bunch of junk when he should have had a decent airplane. Arnold never gave Miff Harmon one iota of credit."
>
> *General Nathan F. Twining, January 2, 1970*

> "Am glad of the opportunity to send a few words in tribute to 'Miff' Harmon. I know they are inadequate, but then – the way I feel about 'Miff' – nothing anyone can say can do him full justice."
>
> *General Henry H. "Hap" Arnold, February 25, 1947*

In February 1945, Technical Sergeant Samuel L. Maas waited patiently to catch a ride to the United States. With long sought-after furlough papers signed by his beloved commander, Maas walked the flight line that had become his home for the last twenty-eight months. Maas, a permanent member of Lieutenant General Harmon's flight crew, served as an assistant flight engineer on his aircraft named *My Ever Lovin Dove II* which was set to be replaced by a newly arrived loaner aircraft and flight crew.[425]

Figure 25: *My Ever Lovin Dove II*, Harmon's aircraft used extensively throughout the Pacific, retired days prior to his fateful flight. Source: AirHistory.Net Photo Archive.

Maas had logged thousands of hours and nearly a million miles traveling throughout the South Pacific, to and from Hawaii and the United States with *his* General. Responsible for pre-flight checks, refueling, and other routine maintenance functions, Maas temporarily and reluctantly relinquished *Dove II* as a provisional crew on loan to General Harmon, along with a new aircraft had just arrived for the General.[426]

---

425 Sam Maas (surviving member of Millard F. Harmon, Jr. flight crew), interview by the author, 18 April 2007.

426 Helen Harmon Nazzaro (daughter of Millard F. Harmon, Jr.), interview by the author, 19 March 2007.

While waiting for his flight to the states, Maas noticed the temporary flight engineer working on an aircraft space heater with numerous parts in disarray and strewn across the tarmac. He made it a point to investigate and offer his services to the new crewmember. Upon asking the young man if he needed help, the engineer replied, "nope, I have it fixed already, and it's going back in the aircraft right now."[427] The portable aircraft heater was the South Wind Model 789 space heater, a converted automotive device installed on modified aircraft during World War II.[428] Flight at high altitudes on the C-87A, especially during winter, required up to as many as ten of these heaters on board to maintain some semblance of comfort for the crew and passengers. Built in 1935, the space heaters used glow plugs and one hundred-octane fuel to provide a minimal amount of radiant heat for the aircraft. The fuel was supplied to the glow plugs from the aircraft tanks while in flight.[429]

Maas thought nothing more of the encounter until days later, while on leave in Wisconsin when he learned of the horrible accident. That temp plane, along with his General, was missing in the vast Pacific Ocean.[430] It is impossible to determine the root cause for the fatal accident, but it is my assumption that a faulty space heater combined with ambient fuel fumes in the aircraft

---

[427] Sam Maas (surviving member of Millard F. Harmon, Jr. flight crew), interview by the author, 18 April 2007.

[428] Jesse Brooks Mellett, test engineer, South Wind Division, Stewart-Warner, to Samuel L. Maas, letter, 2 February 1990, in the personal collection of Samuel L. Maas, copy in author's personal collection.

[429] Letter, Mellett to Maas, 2 February 1990.

[430] Tragically, four years earlier, while on his observer mission to London, Harmon noted that conditions on board RAF aircraft in the wintertime were terrible. He advocated the use of electrically heated clothing or some other type of heaters on board the aircraft. The very system he recommended, might have been the system that resulted in his death.

possibly resulted in the catastrophic destruction of Harmon's airplane. Search and rescue efforts over the next eighteen days found nothing of the missing flight. An intense midair explosion, in all probability, incinerated the aircraft, leaving no traces for the thousands of personnel involved in the frantic search.

Sam Maas was 93 years old when he passed away in 2008. He was 30 when he left his *Dove II* and crew for some much needed rest, but he spent the remainder of his days, living in Nevada and carrying a terrible burden. Until his death, he questioned his actions on the flight line in February 1945.[431] Should he have told someone about the heater repair work, or should he have insisted on the temporary crew installing a brand-new heater? Since that event in 1945 until his passing, sleeping only with the aid of medications, Maas lit a candle in commemoration of the day Harmon and his crew, many of whom were his friends, went missing over the Pacific.[432] To this day, nothing has ever been found from the missing aircraft.

From West Point to the Western Pacific

Of the many lessons that can be learned by studying Harmon's legacy, three main themes resonate. First, Harmon had an incredible ability to foster relationships and build effective teams during the most trying times. Harmon's staff selections in July 1942 worried many in the War Department, particularly General George Marshall. Harmon selected mostly Air Force officers to accompany him to Noumea as the initial cadre of an organization built primarily

---

[431] Sam Maas, interview by the author, 18 April 2007.

[432] One of the most memorable moments during my research of Harmon was a phone interview I had with Sam Maas before he passed. Like many World War II veterans I have met, the details of key events from decades ago, were as sharp as if they had happened the day prior.

to secure Army interests in the Navy theater. Yet despite Marshall's protests, Harmon's astute judgment of character and his grand leadership allowed him to create an organization that weathered, and eventually flourished in the grim periods of 1942.

From that initial staff, many of Harmon's selections rose to high positions in the Air Force. Dean C. "Doc" Strother, Harmon's operations officer for fighters, eventually became a full General and commanded the North American Air Defense Command (NORAD). Frank F. Everest, Harmon's operations officer for bombers, rose to the rank of full General and commanded the United States Air Forces in Europe (USAFE) and Tactical Air Command (TAC). Harmon's trusted advisor for all air operations, initially serving as his Chief of Staff, Nathan F. Twining achieved full General and served as the Chief of Staff of the United States Air Force and eventually became the Chairman of the Joint Chiefs of Staff (CJCS). Clearly General Harmon saw potential and leadership in his young officers well before others and his authenticity, approachable leadership style and humility instilled confidence in his subordinates and created highly effective teams.

Harmon's ability to foster solid relationships outside of his service paid immense dividends. Harmon earned the respect and confidence of many of the senior Navy leaders of the Pacific, specifically Admirals Halsey and Nimitz. On several occasions, Halsey referred to Harmon as his personal "Rock of Gibraltar." Halsey relied on Harmon's expertise and sage advice during their combined push through the Solomons. In return, Halsey supported Harmon's promotion to Lieutenant General and awarded him the Navy's Distinguished Service Medal (DSM) over twelve months before the Army awarded Harmon a similar medal.[433] Harmon's Navy DSM reads as follows: "Demonstrating exceptional initiative and capability in organizing, planning, and commanding his forces, Lieutenant General Harmon contributed immeasurably to the success of the Solomon Islands Campaign. His inspiring leadership, tireless devotion to duty, and earnest cooperation set an effective example to all forces in the South Pacific Area and were in keeping with the highest traditions of the United States Armed Forces."[434]

Halsey commented to Dean Strother on the day Harmon was lost at sea that Harmon was the "craziest little guy that ever lived."[435] "God Damn," Halsey proclaimed, "he's the craziest little guy." He further wrote on Harmon's passing that he "exhibited the finest qualities of a courageous leader, a brilliant tactician, and true patriot. I regard his passing as a great personal loss."[436]

Nimitz spoke at the dedication of Harmon Field on Guam and said Harmon "showed himself to be a great military leader."[437]

---

[433] The Army awarded Harmon the Distinguished Service Medal on 5 July 1944 for the period covering August 1941 to July 1944. The Navy awarded Harmon the Distinguished Service Medal on 19 May 1943, nearly fourteen months earlier. Even the British recognized Harmon's efforts presenting him with the "Honorary Member of the Military Division of the Third Class or Companions of our said Most Honorable Order of the Bath" on 5 February 1945. Incidentally, Hap Arnold received an Army DSM from Brigadier General George Stratemeyer upon the conclusion of his fourteen-day trip around the South Pacific in 1942.
[434] Citation, Distinguished Service Medal (Navy), Frank Knox, Secretary of the Navy, Millard F. Harmon, III. Copy in author's personal collection.
[435] Oral History Interview of General Dean C. Strother by Dr. Edgar F. Puryear, Jr., 9 April 1976. Typed transcript, p. 14, K239.0512-1492, IRIS No. 01053456, in USAF Collection, AFHRA.
[436] Fleet Admiral W.F. Halsey, United States Navy, to Major General A.V. Arnold, War Department, letter, 24 February 1947, Library of Congress, H.H. Arnold Papers, microfilm 28064, reel 26, folder 252.
[437] Nimitz, Address.

Figure 26: Halsey awarding Harmon the Navy DSM. Source: Dr. Thomas Hughes. Picture in author's personal collection.

He "understood air power and employed it with imagination and courage."[438] Furthermore, Nimitz highlighted Harmon's realization of the "necessity for close cooperation among all branches of the service."[439] "He appreciated the strength that lies in unity of purpose and action," feeling "at home on the bridge of an aircraft carrier as in one of his heavy bombers."[440] Nimitz lamented that

[438] Nimitz, Address.
[439] Nimitz, Address.
[440] Nimitz, Address.

Harmon would not be present as the Americans went "forward to inevitable victory."[441]

Harmon also had a common touch, earning a great deal of respect from the enlisted men under his command. In one particular situation, Harmon found the Post Exchange (PX) at one of his bases had made a profit of $700 on nearly $700,000 of gross revenue.[442] Harmon questioned the PX pricing practices stating PX's were not in the business of making money from the fighting men in the Pacific. On another occasion, Harmon issued a general order giving enlisted men unlimited free coffee. Normally a rationed product overseas, coffee was a requirement for troops working long shifts into the night. This general order maddened the supply officers but had a "whale of an effect on the morale of the men."[443]

Harmon leveraged many of the relationships he made during his thirty years of service. Alongside men such as Stratemeyer, Spaatz, Arnold, and Marshall, Harmon worked hard to negotiate the incredibly difficult command positions he held. No person without the interpersonal skills, expertise, and trustworthiness of Miff Harmon would have achieved the success he did in the Pacific theater. Commanding the complex and divergent organizations he faced in World War II required a rare leader.

---

[441] Nimitz, Address.

[442] "General Harmon," *Brief Magazine*, 27 March 1945, in Millard F. Harmon Papers, 702.952-4, IRIS No. 001083064, AFHRA.

[443] "General Harmon," *Brief Magazine*.

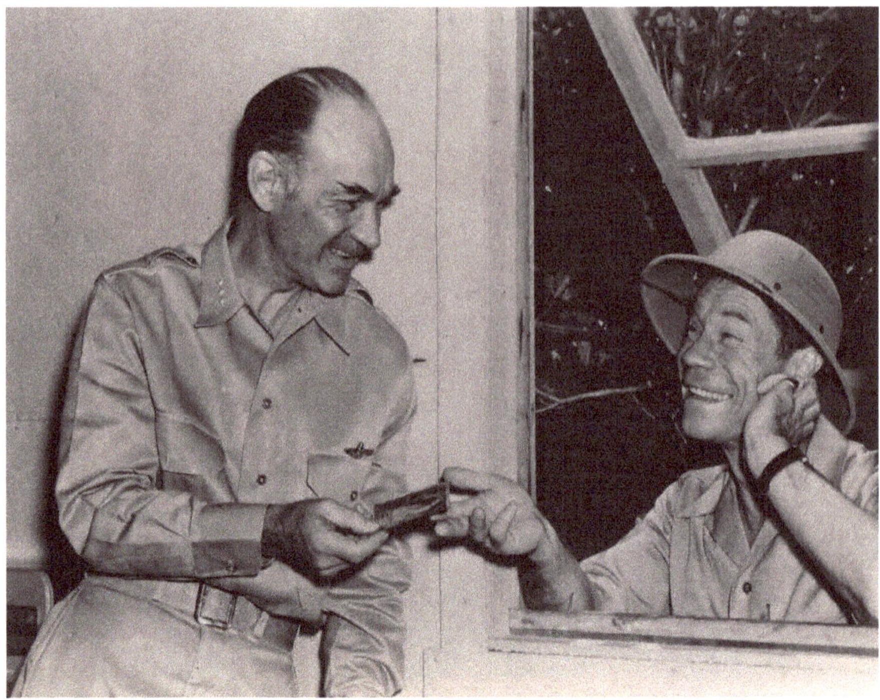

Figure 27: Harmon and comedian Joe E. Brown. The two men exchange a "short snorter bill" during a USO visit to the Pacific in 1944. Source: Millard F. Harmon, III. Picture in author's personal collection.

Power of Joint Operations

The second theme weaving throughout Harmon's career is combined and joint actions. Harmon noted from a very early age the need to create organizations and planning staffs that focused on joint operations. From his early exploits on the Punitive Expedition, joint exercises in Panama and Hawaii to his efforts in the South and Central Pacific Theaters, Harmon stressed the need to coordinate the independent strengths of each service for the achievement of the common good. Harmon viewed many of the ongoing service practices as roadblocks to achieving victory for the nation. In almost every after-action report or lessons-learned memorandum, Harmon noted the need to streamline planning efforts, increase liaison officer billets and reduce independent supply efforts in favor of a joint procurement program. Even today, the armed forces of the United States work to improve these very issues.

"Strategic Tenacity"

Harmon's final strength was his 'strategic tenacity.' Throughout his experiences in World War II, Harmon faced a vicious enemy in the Japanese. At the same time, Harmon had to navigate through the milieu of military bureaucracy and political entanglements that were by-products of an ongoing war in Washington, DC. At every step along the way, Harmon never lost his focus as a combat commander, yet he was generally able to pilot productively through the constant pitfalls of his command.

Upon arrival in the South Pacific, Harmon recognized that planning efforts and operational details were insufficient. Harmon knew early on that the South Pacific fight could be won only with the application of airpower. Naval airpower in the form of carrier aviation was still reeling from the losses at Midway, Coral Sea, and the Solomons. Therefore, the acquisition of multiple airfields from which land-based airpower could operate became the focus of Harmon's efforts. Saddled with Navy control over his own aircraft, Harmon worked with McCain and Fitch, convincing them of the proper use of Army Air Forces assets. Harmon also succeeded in establishing the Thirteenth Air Force, balancing the Navy's operational control and instituting some unity of command and concentrated effort.

Throughout this period, Harmon constantly prodded supply organizations, the Army Air Forces, the Navy, and the War Department to rush more aircraft and men to his theater. After receiving approval from General Marshall, Harmon intercepted P-

38 fighter aircraft enroute to MacArthur's theater and kept them for his own units. Harmon never gave up the fight for Guadalcanal. Even in the face of Admiral Ghormley's decision to invade Ndeni, Harmon maintained the effort would violate the principles of security and possibly sacrifice all of Guadalcanal. Upon Ghormley's removal, Harmon immediately convinced Halsey to abort the operation.

Harmon showed great 'strategic tenacity' regarding subsequent decisions in the Solomons Campaign. As officers senior to Harmon contemplated bypassing the Russells or even New Georgia, Harmon outlined the dangers of those plans and won approval for his scheme of maneuver. Harmon eventually had a direct hand in the operational and tactical successes on New Georgia and Bougainville. In a similar scenario, Nimitz favored the invasion of Formosa as a preferred staging location for B-29 aircraft. Yet, Harmon wholeheartedly disagreed, fearing a massive bloodletting at the hands of the Japanese. Harmon wrote that he was "not in accord with the strategic concept of CAUSEWAY."[444] Furthermore, he felt the invasion of Formosa would be like "sticking our head in a noose."[445] Eventually, Admiral Nimitz and the JCS canceled plans for Formosa, instead choosing Okinawa, one of Harmon's recommendations.

During many periods of World War II, it is evident from correspondence that Harmon's vigorous efforts and constant prodding of outside agencies angered many senior leaders. Harmon frustrated Arnold on many occasions regarding the P-400

---

[444] Lieutenant General M.F. Harmon, Deputy Commander, Twentieth Air Force, to Brigadier General H.S. Hansell, Chief of Staff, Twentieth Air Force, letter, 25 August 1944, in Personal Collection of Gen Henry H. Arnold, MICFILM 28079, AFHRA.

[445] Harmon to Hansell, 25 August 1944.

/ P-38 debate in the South Pacific or the command arrangements of the Twentieth Air Force. Harmon undoubtedly worried Marshall with his selection of nearly all Air Force officers for his initial staff or his policies as USAFISPA. Nimitz questioned Harmon's decision to fire Hester on New Georgia and grappled with Harmon numerous times regarding VHB construction priorities. Yet, in all of the heated discussions and furious letter writings, no one ever removed Harmon from his position. Senior leaders were fired on many occasions in the Pacific theater, as even a cursory glance at the careers of Ghormley, Hester, and Hansell indicates. Still, Harmon retained command billets and, if anything, continually increased his own sphere of influence. In the tangled web of command relationships, where one man reported to so many different authorities, it is remarkable that Harmon produced such impressive results.

Arnold and Harmon

Nathan Twining's remarks, accusing Hap Arnold of ignoring Harmon and contributing to his death through neglect, maybe a bit strident. Endless cries for men and materials from all corners confronted Arnold throughout the entire war, creating significant conflicting interests. Harmon and Twining fought strenuously for their theater, pushing Arnold for action. At the same time, Arnold had to balance these against many of the same demands heard from Spaatz and Eaker in Europe and the Mediterranean. The world was at war, and everywhere Americans were attempting to solve crisis after crisis. Regrettably, the South Pacific Theater suffered, not simply because Arnold intended it, but because the strategic decision made by the President and the JCS put Germany first. If Guadalcanal had not turned for the worse in fall 1942, thereby capturing President Roosevelt's full attention, the supply situation in the Solomons might never have been solved.

Still, Harmon failed to receive due recognition from Arnold and the nation's air arm. Arnold's lack of gratitude may be attributable to his gruff personality or simply procrastination. But to claim that Arnold did not appreciate Harmon's great accomplishments during the war is incorrect. A eulogy letter by Hap Arnold, written in the calm of 1947, clearly speaks of Arnold's incredible respect for Miff Harmon. Arnold wrote that during times of great crises, the country produces great leaders who find themselves "where they belong."[446] Miff Harmon found himself "as one of the best of our great air leaders," he wrote. It was clear from the beginning that Harmon would become "one of the world's outstanding airmen and one of the Army's best generals."[447] Harmon had a "rare gift" that allowed him to secure the "loyalty from all members of his command with no apparent effort."[448] Arnold wrote that he "leaned on him, recognized his ability, counted upon his doing those tough jobs that can be accomplished only when a man has the confidence and loyalty of those above, as well as of those below him."[449] Arnold concluded: "to us of the Army Air Forces, he was more than just another officer; more than a remarkable air expert who always looked far into the future; a capable general whose ability always outranked the difficulty of any given assignment. To us, he was, above all else, a true friend. That is why we miss him so sincerely. That is why we shall never forget him."[450]

---

[446] General H.H. Arnold, USAAF Retired, to Major General A.V. Arnold, Chief, Plans Section, AGF, letter, 17 February 1947, in H.H. Arnold Papers, MICFILM 28064, index 839, reel 26, frame 737, folder 252, Library of Congress, Washington, DC.
[447] H.H. Arnold to A.V. Arnold, 17 February 1947.
[448] H.H. Arnold to A.V. Arnold, 17 February 1947.
[449] H.H. Arnold to A.V. Arnold, 17 February 1947.
[450] H.H. Arnold to A.V. Arnold, 17 February 1947.

Lost in History

Millard F. Harmon, Jr. was all of those things--a remarkable leader, a pioneer aviator, and an organizer of men par excellence. In peacetime, Harmon reorganized the professional military education system for all air officers. He advocated continued study in preparation for the fast pace of airpower advancement, confident that the Air Force would achieve independence sooner rather than later. A keen eye to the future, Miff used his time in Mexico or England to study, plan and document the painful lessons he witnessed. Harmon's labors in the Pacific Theater built the foundation upon which rested many of the great successes of other men. Were it not for Harmon's quick action, Guadalcanal may have been lost. Were it not for Harmon's ingenuity, bombing tactics in the South Pacific could have stagnated. Were it not for Harmon's organizational skills and forethought; the VHB program might have faltered. In the end, he molded a cadre of future leaders who would lead the Air Force and the nation through even more troubling times. Yet, with all of these achievements, Harmon remains a footnote in many historical documents. History reflects fondly upon air leaders such as Mitchell, Doolittle, Spaatz and LeMay, men trained as airmen who fought great air wars. Harmon was also trained as an airman, yet fought a land and air war, all within a naval theater.

Millard F. Harmon, Jr. stands today as a model for the modern leader. He was a man of conviction whose loyalty to his men and his country served as a beacon of light during the darkest days of war. Harmon was an expert in his weapon system, a leader who constantly studied the military arts and tried to capture valuable lessons that others might appreciate in the future. He lobbied for joint exercises and realistic training in peacetime and the power of the offensive in wartime. Focused on winning his nation's wars, Miff Harmon achieved his mission with style, grace, and integrity.

Bibliography

Books

Appleman, Roy E., James M. Burns, Russell A. Gugeler, and John Stevens. *United States Army in World War II. The War in the Pacific. Okinawa: The Last Battle*. New imprint, Washington, DC: Center of Military History, United States Army, 1993.

Arnold, Gen H. H. *Global Mission*. New York, NY: Harper & Brothers, 1949.

Craven, Wesley Frank, and James Lea Cate, eds. *The Army Air Forces in World War II.* 7 vols. 1948-1958. New imprint, Washington, DC: Office of Air Force History, 1983.

_______. *The Army Air Forces in World War II*. Vol. 4, *The Pacific – Guadalcanal to Saipan, August 1942 to July 1944*. 1949. New imprint, Washington, DC: Office of Air Force History, 1983.

_______. *The Army Air Forces in World War II*. Vol. 5, *The Pacific – Matterhorn to Nagasaki, June 1944 to August 1945*. Chicago, IL: University of Chicago Press, 1953.

Davis, Burke. *The Billy Mitchell Affair*. New York: Random House, 1967.

Doolittle, James H. and Carroll V. Glines. *I Could Never Be So Lucky Again: An Autobiography by General James H. "Jimmy" Doolittle*. New York: Bantam Books, 1991.

Griffith, Samuel B., II. *The Battle for Guadalcanal.* Philadelphia: J.B. Lippincott Co., 1963

Halsey, Fleet Admiral William F., and Lieutenant Commander J. Bryan III. Admiral *Halsey's Story*. New York, NY: Whittlesey House, 1947.

Huston, John W. *America's Airpower Comes of Age: General Henry H. "Hap" Arnold's World War II Diaries*. Maxwell AFB, AL: Air University Press, 2002.

Johnson, Herbert A. *U.S. Army Aviation through World War I*. Chapel Hill, NC: The University of North Carolina Press, 2001.

Kenney, George C. *General Kenney Reports: A Personal History of the Pacific War.* New York: Duell, Sloan and Pearce, 1949.

Larrabee, Eric. *Commander in Chief: Franklin Delano Roosevelt, His Lieutenants, and Their War*. New York, NY: Simon & Schuster Inc., 1987.

Linn, Brian McAllister. *The Philippine War: 1899-1902*. Lawrence, KS: University of Kansas Press, 2000.

Miller, John, Jr. *United States Army in World War II. The War in the Pacific. Guadalcanal: The First Offensive*. Washington, DC: Historical Division, Department of the Army, 1949.

_______. *United States Army in World War II. The War in the Pacific. Cartwheel: The Reduction of Rabaul*. Washington, DC: Office of the Chief of Military History, 1959.

Mitchell, William. *Winged Defense: The Development and Possibilities of Modern Air Power – Economic and Military*. Mineola, NY: Dover Publications Inc., 2006.

Morrison, Samuel Eliot. *Breaking the Bismarcks Barrier, 22 July 1942-1 May 1944*. Boston, MA: Little, Brown and Company, 1950.

Morton, Louis. *United States Army in World War II. The War in the Pacific. Strategy and Command: The First Two Years*. 1962.

New imprint, Washington, DC: Center for Military History, United States Army, 2000.

Potter, E. B. *Nimitz*. Annapolis, MD: Naval Institute Press, 1976.

Periodicals

Classmates. "Millard Fillmore Harmon, Jr.," *Assembly*, Association of Graduates, United States Military Academy, West Point Alumni Foundation, 7, no. 2 (July 1948): 12 – 14.

Ferguson, Robert L. "General Millard F. Harmon," *Military* 19, no. 6 (November 2002): 6 – 11.

_______. "General Millard F. Harmon," *Military* 19, no. 7 (December 2002): 12 – 16.

Hines, Calvin W. "First Aero Squadron in Mexico," A*merican Aviation Historical Journal* 10, no. 3 (3rd Quarter 1965): 190 – 197.

"Meet Colonel Harmon," *Form One* 1, no. 4 (September 1940): 4 – 18.

Saltsman, Ralph H. "The 67th Fighter Squadron, "Fighting Cocks" at Guadalcanal," *Air Power History* 47, no. 4 (Winter 2000): 46 – 49.

Searle, Thomas R. "'It Made a Lot of Sense to Kill Skilled Workers': The Firebombing of Tokyo in March 1945," *The Journal of Military History* 66, no. 1 (January 2002): 103 – 134.

Newspaper Items

New York Times, 23 March 1943

New York Times, 23 April 1943

New York Times, 1 September 1944

New York Times, 27 November 1944

New York Times, 4 March 1945

New York Times, 8 May 1945

Historical Studies

Finney, Robert T. *History of the Air Corps Tactical School, 1920-1940*. USAF Historical Study 100. Maxwell AFB, AL: USAF Historical Division, Air University, 1955.

Greer, Thomas H. *The Development of Air Doctrine in the Army air arm, 1917-1941*. USAF Special Studies. 1955. New imprint, Washington, DC: Office of Air Force History, 1985.

Hennessy, Juliette A. *The United States Army Air Arm, April 1861 to April 1917*, USAF Historical Study 98. Maxwell AFB, AL: USAF Historical Division, Air University, 1958.

Reports

Harmon, Maj M.F., "Carnet d' Emploi du Temps," 1918 – 1921.

"Report of Search for Lt Gen Millard F. Harmon, USAAF, Commanding General, Army Air Forces, Pacific Oceans Areas." March 1945.

Unpublished Papers

Andress, Steven. "The Forgotten General." Unpublished article, Winnetka, CA, 2001.

Letters

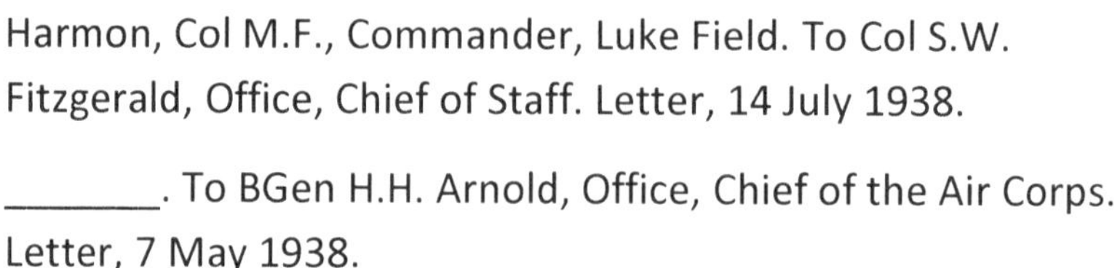

Harmon, Col M.F., Commander, Luke Field. To Col S.W. Fitzgerald, Office, Chief of Staff. Letter, 14 July 1938.

_______. To BGen H.H. Arnold, Office, Chief of the Air Corps. Letter, 7 May 1938.

_______. To Maj Gen O.Westover, Chief of the Air Corps. Letter, 30 June 1938.

Chennault, C.L. To Col M.F. Harmon, Assistant Commandant, Air Corps Tactical School. Letter, 28 July 1939.

Stratemeyer, LtCol G.E., Office of the Chief of the Air Corps. To Col M.F. Harmon, Assistant Commandant, Air Corps Tactical School. Letter, 22 July 1939.

Harmon, Col M.F., Assistant Commandant, Air Corps Tactical School. To Brig Gen B.K. Yount. Letter, 25 November 1939.

_______. To Maj Gen H.H. Arnold, Chief of the Air Corps. Letter, 9 October 1939.

Marshall, Gen G.C., Chief of Staff, War Department. To Col M.F. Harmon, Assistant Commandant, Air Corps Tactical School. Letter, 26 January 1940.

Harmon, Col M.F., Assistant Commandant, Air Corps Tactical School. To Gen G.C. Marshall, Chief of Staff, War Department. Letter, 30 January 1940.

_______. To Gen G.C. Marshall, Chief of Staff, War Department. Draft Letter, no date.

_______. To Col C.H. Hodges, Assistant Commandant, The Infantry School. Letter, 30 January 1940.

Arnold, Maj Gen H.H., Chief of the Air Corps. To Col C.H. Hodges, Assistant Commandant, The Infantry School. Letter, 30 January 1940.

_______. To Col M.F. Harmon, Assistant Commandant, Air Corps Tactical School. Letter, 1 February 1940.

Harmon, Col M.F., Assistant Commandant, Air Corps Tactical School. To Maj Gen H.H. Arnold, Chief of the Air Corps. Letter, 5 February 1940.

Arnold, Lt Gen H.H., Chief of the Air Corps. To Maj Gen M.F. Harmon, Chief of Staff, Chief of the Air Corps. Letter, 10 March 1941.

McCain, RADM J.S., Commander, Air South Pacific. To VADM R.L. Ghormley, Commander, South Pacific. Letter, 6 July 1942.

Nimitz, ADM C.W., Commander in Chief, Pacific. To RADM J.S. McCain, Commander, Air, South Pacific. Letter, 27 July 1942.

Ghormley, VADM R.L., Commander, South Pacific. To ADM C.W. Nimitz, Commander in Chief, Pacific. Letter, 29 July 1942.

_______. To ADM C.W. Nimitz, Commander in Chief, Pacific. Letter, 11 August 1942.

Arnold, Lt Gen H.H., Commanding General, Army Air Forces. To Maj Gen C.A. Spaatz, Commanding General, Eighth Air Force. Letter, 19 August 1942.

Spaatz, Maj Gen C.A., Commanding General, Eighth Air Force. To BGen G.E. Stratemeyer, Chief of Staff, Commanding General, Army Air Forces. Letter, 21 August 1942.

_______. To Gen H.H. Arnold, Commanding General, Army Air Forces. Letter, 31 August 1942.

Ghormley, VADM R.L., Commander, South Pacific. To ADM C.W. Nimitz, Commander in Chief, Pacific. Letter, 7 September 1942.

McCain, RADM J.S., Commander, Air South Pacific. To RADM A.W. Fitch and Maj Gen M.F. Harmon. Letter, 19 September 1942.

Harmon, Maj Gen M.F., Commanding General, United States Army Forces in the South Pacific Area. To VADM R.L. Ghormley, Commander, South Pacific. Letter, 6 October 1942.

_______. To Gen G.C. Marshall, Chief of Staff, War Department. Letter, 17 October 1942.

_______. To Gen H.H. Arnold, Commanding General, Army Air Forces. Letter, 20 October 1942.

Halsey, VADM W.F., Commander, South Pacific. To ADM C.W. Nimitz, Commander in Chief, Pacific. Letter, 31 October 1942.

Harmon, Maj Gen M.F., Commanding General, United States Army Forces in the South Pacific Area. To Gen G.C. Marshall, Chief of Staff, War Department. Letter, 1 November 1942.

Halsey, VADM W.F., Commander, South Pacific. To ADM C.W. Nimitz, Commander in Chief, Pacific. Letter, 6 November 1942.

Harmon, Maj Gen M.F., Commanding General, United States Army Forces in the South Pacific Area. To Gen G.C. Marshall, Chief of Staff, War Department. War Department Message, 6 December 1942.

Halsey, VADM W.F., Commander, South Pacific. To ADM C.W. Nimitz, Commander in Chief, Pacific. Letter, 8 December 1942.

Marshall, Gen G.C., Chief of Staff, War Department. To Maj Gen M.F. Harmon, Commanding General, United States Army Forces in the South Pacific Area. Letter, 8 December 1942.

Nimitz, ADM C.W., Commander in Chief, Pacific. To VADM W.F. Halsey, Commander, South Pacific. Letter, 8 August 1943.

Halsey, VADM W.F., Commander South Pacific. To ADM C.W. Nimitz, Commander in Chief, Pacific. Letter, 19 August 1943.

Harmon, Lt Gen M.F., Commanding General, United States Army Forces in the South Pacific Area. To VADM W.F. Halsey, Commander, South Pacific. Letter, 5 November 1943.

Griswold, Maj Gen O.W., Commanding General, XIV Corps. To Lt Gen M.F. Harmon, Commanding General, United States Army Forces in the South Pacific Area. Letter, 25 April 1944.

Marshall, Gen G.C., Chief of Staff, War Department. To Commanding General, Central Pacific Area and Commanding General, South Pacific Area. Letter, 10 July 1944.

Harmon, Lt Gen M.F., Commanding General, Army Air Forces Pacific Oceans Area. To Gen H.H. Arnold, Commanding General, Army Air Forces. Letter, 15 August 1944.

_______. To Brig Gen H.S. Hansell, Chief of Staff, Twentieth Air Force. Letter, 25 August 1944.

Arnold, Gen H.H., Commanding General, Army Air Forces. To Lt Gen M.F. Harmon, Commanding General, Army Air Forces Pacific Oceans Area. Letter, 25 September 1944.

Giles, Lt Gen B.M., Chief of Staff, Army Air Forces. To Lt Gen M.F. Harmon, Commanding General, Army Air Forces Pacific Oceans Area. Letter, 26 September 1944.

Rosenblatt, Col S., Air Corps. To Maj Gen C.E. LeMay, Commanding General, Twentieth Air Force. Letter, 10 January 1945.

LeMay, Maj Gen C.E., Commanding General, Twentieth Air Force. To Brig Gen L. Norstad, Chief of Staff, Twentieth Air Force. Letter, 31 January 1945.

Rosenblatt, Col S., Air Corps. To Maj Gen C.E. LeMay, Commanding General, Twentieth Air Force. Letter, 23 February 1945.

Arnold, Gen H.H., United States Army Air Forces, retired. To Maj Gen A.V. Arnold, Chief, Plans, AGF. Letter, 17 February 1947.

Halsey, FLTADM W.F., United States Navy. To Maj Gen A.V. Arnold, Chief, Plans, AGF. Letter, 24 February 1947.

Mellett, J.B., Test Engineer, South Wind Division, Stewart-Warner. To S.L. Maas. Letter, 2 February 1990.

Memorandums

Arnold, Gen H.H., Chief of the Air Corps. To Gen G.C. Marshall, Chief of Staff, War Department. Memorandum, "North African Operations." 19 August 1942.

Brant, Brig Gen B.C., Commander, Third Wing. To Commanding General, General Headquarters Air Force. Memorandum, 14 March 1936.

Harmon, Col M.F., Assistant Commandant, Air Corps Tactical School. Memorandum, "Policy for Future Military Education of Air Corps Officers, Preliminary Rough Draft." 15 June 1939.

Harmon, Lt Gen M.F., Commanding General, United States Army Forces in the South Pacific Area. Memorandum for USAFISPA Chief of Staff (handwritten). 28 July 1943.

_______. Memorandum to subordinate USAFISPA commanders. 24 January 1944.

Summaries, Diaries, Minutes, Notes

Foulois, B.D., Commander, First Aero Squadron. "Report of Operations of the First Aero Squadron, Signal Corps, with Punitive Expedition." 28 August 1916.

Green, Dr. Murray. "AAF Operates Under Navy Command in South Pacific – Sept 1942," The Murray Green Collection, US Air Force Academy Library, Colorado Springs, CO.

_______. "Suitability of the P-400 and P-39 – September 1942," The Murray Green Collection, US Air Force Academy Library, Colorado Springs, CO.

_______. "General Harmon's Split Command," The Murray Green Collection, US Air Force Academy Library, Colorado Springs, CO.

Halsey, ADM W.F., Commander, South Pacific. "South Pacific Campaign – Narrative Account." 3 September 1944.

Harmon, Maj M.F., Air Service. "Notes of trip to the French Front in the Region of Chalons sur-Marne – June 1917." June 1917.

Harmon, LtCol M.F., Air Service. "Untitled notes regarding a Topographical survey of Panama." Ca. 1919.

Harmon, Maj Gen M.F., Chief of Staff, Chief of Air Corps. "Diary of General Harmon for Mrs. Harmon – 1941." 18 January 1941 to 31 March 1941.

Harmon, Maj Gen M.F., Commanding General, United States Army Forces in the South Pacific Area. "Narrative – Notes on Bases of the Army, South Pacific (exclusive of Bora Bora, Tongatabu, etc)." 11 August 1942.

_______. "Lessons Learned from Joint Operations in the New Georgia and Bougainville Operations." 5 February 1944.

_______. "The Army in the South Pacific." 6 June 1944.

Proceedings. Board of officers convened in the office, Chief of the Air Corps. 19 April 1939.

Transcript. "Notes on Conference held aboard U.S.S *Argonne* at Noumea." 28 September 1942.

Addresses

Nimitz, ADM C.W., Commander in Chief, Pacific. "Dedication of Harmon Field." Address. Harmon Field, Guam, 8 May 1945.

Electronic Publications

Air and Space Power Journal Online. "Mexican Punitive Expedition." http://www.airpower.maxwell.af.mil/airchronicles/apj/apj02/win02/notam4.pdf (accessed 4 February 2007).

Arlington National Cemetery Website. "Harold Melville Clark, Major, United States Army Air Service." http://www.arlingtoncemetery.net/hmclark.htm (accessed 10 February 2007).

Dictionary of American Naval Fighting Ships. "*McCawley*." http://www.history.navy.mil/danfs/m//mccawley-ii.htm (accessed 15 April 2007).

United States Military Academy Online Archives. "Official Register for the Officers and Cadets, United States Military Academy for 1912." http://digital-library.usma.edu/libmedia/archives/oroc/v1912.pdf (accessed 20 Jan 2007).

About the Author

Brigadier General Robert Novotny, United States Air Force retired, is a 1992 United States Air Force Academy graduate and career combat fighter pilot. After a brief staff assignment at Hickam Air Force Base near Honolulu, Rob was selected for pilot training in 1995, graduating a year later as the Distinguished Graduate from his pilot class with a coveted F-15C Eagle assignment to Langley AFB, Virginia. While at Langley in the 71st Fighter Squadron "Ironmen," Novotny won numerous awards such as Wingman of the Year and Flight Lead of the Year honors on his way towards upgrading to Instructor Pilot. Following Langley, the Air Force assigned Novotny to Kadena AB, Japan, as an Instructor Pilot and selected him to attend the USAF Weapons School analogous to the US Navy's TOP GUN program. Again, Novotny was the #1 graduate of his F-15C class after which he returned to Japan. During Operation Iraqi Freedom in the Spring of 2003, Novotny was the Chief of Weapons & Tactics for the 67th Fighter Squadron "Fighting Cocks" and led numerous missions over Iraq as Mission Commander and Defensive Counter Air Package Commander where he earned multiple combat decorations and flew over 500 combat hours in the F-15C. Following an assignment to the 422d Test and Evaluation Squadron as the Chief, F-15C Operational Test Division, he attended the Naval War College, Newport, Rhode Island, and graduated in 2006 again as a Distinguished Graduate. Rob returned to Kadena AB as the Director of Operations for the 67th Fighter Squadron before taking command of the decorated F-15 squadron in 2008. After his command posting, he was selected for Colonel and attended the National War College before returning to Nellis AFB in Las Vegas to command the bulk of the fighter, bomber, rescue, and unmanned test activities. Requested by name, Rob deployed to Afghanistan as the Chief of Staff for the air component and joint air forces where he was presented the NATO Meritorious Service Medal and the Bronze Star for his service. He then took command of Europe's largest fighter operation, the 48th Fighter Wing known as the "Liberty Wing." During his tenure, he led the wing through massive mission changes and oversaw three Presidentially-authorized strikes into Libya neutralizing over 75 ISIS fighters who were destined for Western European targets. For their combined leadership, Rob and his wife won the Jerome F. O'Malley Trophy for the outstanding wing command team in Europe in 2015. Shortly thereafter, Rob was promoted to Brigadier General and served in the Pentagon and Air Combat Command staffs before returning "home" to Nellis to command the storied 57th Wing. Rob led the massive wing through reorganizations, RED FLAG exercises, Weapons School classes, while revitalizing the US Air Force Thunderbirds after several accidents and a fatality. Rob and the Thunderbirds created what became the "America Strong" fly-bys as the Navy Blue Angels and the Thunderbirds crisscrossed the US during the opening months of the COVID-19 Pandemic. After nearly 29 years on Active Duty, Rob retired and is chasing new dreams...including the completion of this short story.

www.ingramcontent.com/pod-product-compliance
Ingram Content Group UK Ltd.
Pitfield, Milton Keynes, MK11 3LW, UK
UKHW062302290726
14090UKWH00017B/847